Self Aware

Gilbert Schultz

Self Aware

January 2019

Copyright©2019gilbertschultz
All rights reserved. This book, or any portion thereof may not be reproduced or used in any manner whatsoever without the express written permission of the publisher except for the use of brief quotations in a book review. First Printing in Australia and the United States of America.

Editor: Julie Rumbarger

Index

3	Self Aware	77	Freedom Flows
5	Introduction	79	A Fresh Clearing
7	Key Words	84	Nothing Else
10	Your Own Light	87	Gods and Gurus
11	The Message	89	Ever Present
15	Conceptual self	94	No Effort
17	Presence Awareness	99	Radical Leap
20	Time-Mind	102	Attuned
25	Wakefulness	104	Direct Experience
27	Get This Clear	105	Open
29	Confusion	109	Intelligence
30	Nucleus	112	Recognition
33	I Am That	113	Space of Knowing
37	Do Not Doubt	115	Chronologically
39	Psychological Fixation	118	Hammered
45	The Paradox	121	Stories
47	Innately Present	124	Singular
52	Coercion	126	Erroneous Bondage
54	No Owner	129	Investigate
57	Right Here	130	Ever Fresh View
62	Knowing	136	Shining...Mind
64	Reality	139	Enlightenment
65	Bird In Flight	140	Flow
71	Who Knows?	142	See-Know-Be
73	Light	143	Epilogue
		148	Your Notes

Self-Aware

Everything is energy. Nothing can exist without energy. The intelligence that directs the attention back to Presence-Awareness is free of all erroneous beliefs. Insight is a fleeting moment of clear seeing. Awareness itself is **Self-Aware. That is the self.**

No surrendering. No asserting. No worship. Nature freely expresses itself without referring to a self centre.

The natural state is wordless and silent. Re-discovering that, is essential--without it, the mind will carry on forever and a day, repeating its narrative about 'me'.

Self centeredness is the cause of psychological suffering. The reason for unhappiness is a fictional self centre.

The Seven Points of Confirmation

1. Confirm you are not unaware.
2. Confirm you did not have to DO anything to be aware.
3. Confirm seeing is happening. You did not have to DO anything to make the seeing happen.
4. Confirm that hearing is happening and that you did not have to DO anything to make the hearing happen.
5. Confirm that the activity of knowing is happening and that you did not have to DO anything to make the knowing happen.
6. Confirm that all this is happening spontaneously without any permission being requested from 'you'.
7. Confirm that where the actual seeing is taking place, there is no thing standing upon anything.

After confirming these 7 points, where does the ego, or the sufferer, enter? Through which sense or through which faculty?

Introduction

In the scheme of things, there appear many who wish to discover their basic true nature.

Few understand that their basic true nature is not hidden in the mind or anywhere else. Pointing happens through words, and yet it is words that obscure the clear and obvious. The single essence expresses itself as everything. Labels appear to divide up this unicity into a myriad of things.

The recognition that comes unexpectedly, and spontaneously, cannot be reduced to words. It is similar to your feelings; we describe our feelings in an approximate fashion but no words can describe a feeling. In the realm of language, what I speak about is that which has been most often overlooked.

We all speak to each other and we imagine that we understand each other, but it may be far from the truth. In other words, if it could be put into words in an exact way, it would have been done 'long ago'.

Down through the ages, there have been a few who have left records of their pointings and they are as fresh today, as the day they were first expressed.

This livingness--life, is spontaneously fresh and new. Fresh expressions appear and disappear spontaneously (before any consequence called thinking).

Most individuals never meet what we loosely call a 'messenger'. The 'true messenger' speaks from an immediate 'knowledge'.

A recognition of what the pointing points to, will clear the mind of belief, and the spontaneous spacious nature of pure Knowing shines of itself.

Key Words

Mind: Mind, is thought, image, and memory, appearing spontaneously in the so-called intimate space commonly called self (me). Mind is time, mind is 'me'.

Belief: Belief is a cluster of ideas that interrupt the natural translation of experiencing. An individual who is belief free, expresses a clear understanding.

Basically, everything is sensation. The body-mind interprets the sensations and labels them from the so-called past, therefore, it cannot be the immediate reality.

Mind appears out of no mind.
Things appear out of no-thing.

Awareness: Mind without content, is Awareness. Awareness is naked cognition without conceptual content. The ancients called it space-like Awareness because Awareness is like space. Space is 'no thing' (not a thing) to the mind. There is Awareness of thought, feeling and all the senses. The senses are not aware of anything. The senses are attributed with qualities, by the mind, via belief.

To be robbed of belief is to be disillusioned. To be without illusion, is to be naked Awareness. Great fortune in being no one.

As soon as you believe you are someone, a person, there is a maintenance regime.

To be spontaneous Being is to be free of concepts about freedom and bondage.

Thinking is spontaneous. The thinker is a fabricated entity.

There is no 'I' that thinks. Thinking appears spontaneously upon consciousness.

The sense, 'I am': Is like a feeling that has an expansiveness from the core of Being (heart), spreading out, and there is a subtle sense of well-being to it. This is the base to it all. The head is a cloud of misunderstanding.

The ego (mind) says, "I Must be able to contribute SOMETHING."

This: It is silent...it is PRESENCE...Pre-sense. It does not speak. The intellect, free of me, can translate for it.

Me: An interference pattern, distorted by beliefs and opinions, images and memories.

What is of the utmost importance is this: This is not about acquiring anything, not about achieving anything....it is simply about RECOGNISING what is ALREADY SO. The mind says "YES BUT......" (mind fixation is ignorance)

Presence: Is silent, wordless.

Wisdom: Overcomes ignorance without effort.

1

Your Own Light

Within this vast, spacious, essence of immediate Knowing, (this essence that you are), there is a natural, peaceful, abiding.

There is light that enters the body. There is light that shines out of the body. These expressions of light must find a balance. Ignorance is a fixation with one expression of light.

This essence ('I am') is complete just as it is.

Stories of a 'return' are just 'stories' since this 'you', this bias that needs to return, is nothing other than the bias of an erroneous belief. Knowing IS!

This light of Knowing, (which is your own light), shines into the darkest recesses of the mind and frees it. It shines out through the eyes and the body. There is vision (of the eyes) and there is seeing. Everything appears in the seeing. Nothing is hidden. The light of Knowing is the healer. The intellect that thinks it sees everything is the illness.

2

The Message
An Overview

The message is simple. The potency of the message, as it is received, attracts the attention of those open to it, and turns the attention subtly back to its own natural, open space, the living source.

Home

It appears to be a 'deliverance home.' This leaves the troubled, imagined realms of a fragmented mind without the energy of belief and so they naturally wither away.

A surprising number of so-called Non-Duality teachings, only address the intellect, the persona (mask). Endless thought patterns bind the intellect into a never ending cyclical "mind maze," of more and more concepts. Even though it is only in the appearance, it keeps the mind actively searching for what it is apparently looking for. It is a preconceived search, seemingly made by a fabricated entity, thought.

Seeing, Being-ness

Seeing is happening quite naturally and is not dependent on a 'seer' or a 'knower'. The message must strike the Being-ness by passing through the habitual, convoluted mental activity.

The message may arrive as the simplicity of a solo bird singing, or as a single sentence in the written or spoken word.

The essence of the message is imbibed directly through a resonance in Being.

Equality permeates THIS moment.

The Intellect

The foundations of belief are consistently challenged as one approaches the heart of it all *through* the intellect. The intellect is tempted by its own apparent egocentric cleverness, as it indulges in some kind of special knowledge. Esoteric knowledge is especially tempting.

Insight

Direct insight is a Realization for the mind, not study.

The Bible says in Ecclesiastes, 12:12:

"Much study is a weariness to the flesh and in the making of books, there is no end…"

The essential nature of Realization is 'Seeing'. Concepts follow the insight.

Obvious

One of the central factors, which make Non-Duality seem so difficult to grasp, is that the Non-Dual nature of everything, is so obvious.

Intellectual Paralysis

The wrangling dis-ease only lasts as long as the fixation with it. The intellect 'appears' to be consistently attracted to complications and to the paradox of conflicting concepts. "Analysis paralysis," is a favorite pastime with seekers. The peaceful moments of no thought are not noticed because they are of **no value to the ego.**

The mind constructions and complications do not actually exist, which means that resolving them is just impossible for mind. They simply vanish.

As Sri Nisargadatta Maharaj is quoted as saying,*"No university can teach you to be yourself."*

Direct, 'Seeing-Knowing', is the means.

Intelligence (energy) eliminates erroneous beliefs the moment they are seen for what they are. The tendency to hold onto beliefs loses its grip on mind.

Is not Self-Realization simply 'Seeing what is'?

The potency of revelation is via the pure function of 'Seeing'. Seeing what is true – is not a belief. At no point, in any 'time', is 'Seeing' not present, not happening.

Pay Attention

My advice is to drop all study and simply pay attention to what is. It is simply obvious.

Seeing is not a 'doing' made by any 'entity'. It is that pure functioning happening with you right now. Your 'immediate life' is THIS moment, just as it is.

Let the natural state resonate. The open view will appear to expand quite spontaneously, with no effort being made by anyone.

Do not follow thoughts. All directions are in the mind. They all lead away from the simplicity. All paths lead to unreality.

3

Conceptual 'Self'

Are you prepared to stop pretending to be a spiritual person? Are you willing to BE the pure light of Knowing which shines forth from your own authentic Being? What are you afraid of? Who is afraid?

There is nowhere to hide.

It appears that this conceptual 'you' must face it, in one way or another, but it does not have a face. The psychological aspect, the image of self, seems as if it is hiding from the authenticity because it feels unworthy, impure or whatever.

Acknowledging it is either right here in this now, or dramatically and finally at the end of this story of a separate life--which will be now also. No difference.

Strike with the sword of truth and free yourself from these deluded states of mind, in which you take yourself to be something 'other' than this light of Knowing.

You are the source of light by which you See everything. In Knowing that, there is no need to face anything, because *you are That*.

I am Awake — Present and Aware.

Can you truly say that you are NOT THIS also?

The free man moves on and adheres to no system. Neither does he fixate on any reference points. He lives entirely within the spontaneous freshness of each unfolding moment, no matter how it may be appearing.

Even the re-appearance of habitual patterns of reference are not binding in this free and open state of Awareness.

4

Presence Awareness

Awareness is space-like. The ancient texts tell us that it is 'space-like Awareness'.

Right THERE, where these very words are registering, via the pure function of Seeing, there is nothing that you can know of as 'something' which is registering all the millions of impressions.

It is not a screen, nor a bunch of brain cells. It is space-like. It is all too obvious, and we normally miss it altogether.

There, in that space-like Awareness, there is an indescribable sense of open space with no boundary to be found anywhere. It has no qualities that one can objectify. One could call it 'clarity', but it is best to leave it nameless.

In this vast open space, the whole world appears, including the body with feelings, sensations, thoughts, states, etc. Nothing alters this space-like Awareness. It is unchanging and timelessly present. It is Presence itself.

Discovering this 'invisible Presence' to be your true nature, somehow mysteriously releases the habitual identified consciousness. One's natural Presence is found to be an ease of Being and totally unencumbered.

In this space-like Awareness, there is no one to have or not have any claim or ownership of it.

It simply is.

It is pure wakefulness – absolutely stable, it is the Un-mediated Knowing Presence - of itself. Everything else appears in THAT and is the movement and the changing – energy – Livingness.

It is through this movement, that 'Knowing' happens. The activity of Knowing is energy movement, and one can realize that everything is this activity of Knowing - no separation.

Everything registers directly and immediately in, or upon, Presence Awareness.

It is too obvious to notice as long as old ideas pervade the mind, and it is impossible to objectively 'see'.

The FACT is: It is the Seeing.

I am That.

The activity of Knowing (cognition) is your true nature. It is not a thing, it never was and never will be. It is the ever-immediate spontaneous cognising.

5

Time--Mind

The true nature of mind is pure empty wakefulness.

The dualistic state of mind is restlessness. It will never be brought to a restful silence by any activity that arises from a fixated point within its own realm. This fact is almost always ignored, or not even suspected by otherwise serious spiritual seekers.

It comes down to clear information. Such clear information is not so available through traditional systems. It is expressed by a small number of clear teachers who almost always insist that they are not a teacher at all. They point you straight back to your own Presence of Being - Seeing - Knowing. Few recognize the significance of this 'pointing'. Such is the apparent depth of identified states of mind. The insubstantial 'fixated hold' on consciousness is due to dualistic states of mind. Along with this, there is a belief in 'time' as being something quite real, "I'll get it later" - "I'll see it eventually!" This is accompanied by attachments to objects, which are believed to be 'in time'.

Are you convinced of the reality of this 'time realm'? Do you believe that you depend on it? The adherence to this belief is widespread and of the common mind. It is rarely investigated. Your beliefs, without exception, are all in 'acquired mind' which is based on a 'dead past'. It can also be called the 'conditioned mind'.

The conditioning of mind belongs in time.

Belief in a 'substantial past' can limit the Presence of mind with all kinds of projections, into some 'future time', which is based on memory and imagination — which are all images from the past.

Everything, without exception, is fictitious in this mind realm of self-hypnosis.

Immediate living-ness, authentic Being, is not time bound. It has no time. One must re-discover this for one-self. It discovers itself via a resonance in its own home ground — authentic pure Being. Not two.

The practical knowledge of daily life is not in question here. This message is addressed directly to authentic Being. It must penetrate through the realm of belief, (psychological suffering) and resonate in immediate Knowing.

The natural clarity of mind is clouded by the restless activity of opinions and beliefs which arise as conditioned responses to stimuli in your world.

All this appears to assist in a survival of the onslaughts of life. If you start to take notice, you will see that all the dramas of life actually depend on 'time'. "So and so did such and such." Past! It is no longer present evidence apart from the constant reference to it in the mind. Give it no attention and see what happens to the drama.

Inner squabbling settles down and the view changes. The actual Present emerges in view and the quality of mind changes. The absence of erroneous beliefs leaves the clear and obvious as it is.

In the appearance of a restless mind, you will find no peace. Squeezing this restless mind into a stern practice of meditation is quite useless, yet so many try so avidly to do this. What is achieved? — Truly?

Meditation intensives are popular, and Enlightenment seminars are everywhere. Thousands upon thousands appear to go by these erroneous paths. They are not necessarily bad things in themselves, but the so-called 'results' are transient and time bound.

Any state which is 'reached' will dissipate naturally.

Attachment to any pattern of energy will itself, inevitably dissolve, along with whatever it is attached to.

Anyone teaching these methods, who proclaims to be enlightened, is 'pulling your leg'. No exceptions! What's more, they know it too. There is no such thing as an enlightened 'person'.

The fact is, that a restless mind cannot be molded into a peaceful state, no matter what practice or method you use. This is an unfavorable statement for many aspirants. Even so, it must be pointed out.

The main point to recognize is that the fixated point of reference called 'me', is the *one* trying to attain liberation. The me is a fiction, and as such, cannot 'do' anything. It cannot know anything, see anything or change anything. It is no different than any other fixation.

It is all a misunderstanding, a conceptualised 'someone' (a bunch of ideas) which appears as an attempt to climb up, go around, or escape from its own structure of reference points — ideas. Liberation is only found in the true nature of mind, which is a clear, open, and natural state of wakefulness. You will never squeeze a restless mind into a peaceful space, so don't try!

The 'one' trying, is the obstacle!

This natural state is unachievable for any 'individual', due to the fact that this individual is a series of reference points, that only appear and disappear in the natural open un-mediated Awareness. **Simple Wakefulness.** Wakefulness is already everpresent. It IS. It is your own true nature. You have never been without it. You cannot alter this timeless fact. Without it, there is nothing but ignorance.

6

Wakefulness

When you look back and see what you were, and what you might have been, are you ignoring what you are right now?

All of our hopes and dreams, our regrets and accomplishments, provide no real shelter from the actuality of this Presence, right now.

Indulgence is a form of ignorance. To believe in this ignorance is a habitual pattern in mind, and what you are cannot be a habit.

You, are the natural Presence only.

The simplicity of Presence (of mind) is the actuality of what is present right now. See that it is so. The attention is like a lens of Awareness. If our focus is narrowed or is turned away from what is clearly evident presently, then we are cast into the imaginary, shadowy realms of the mind — but only because there is belief in these concepts — it's just a habit — a tendency. They are translations and projections of mind.

Start with the acknowledgement, the fact, that you--are already That. Be alert and pay attention to your immediate livingness. Deal with whatever needs to be attended to, from and AS this Presence - Awareness. Clarity of mind is only found right here, right now. Right here, is the only place where the functioning mind is free to navigate through the demands that are arising from all these changing circumstances called LIFE.

Everything registers in this openness. It may be vivid or intense in its freshness. It cannot harm you.

This will settle, as the contrast of previous states of mind fade away. This crispness is always here. It is only covered over by states of mind. Habits of mind are a fog, which will clear away naturally by itself. Do not follow thoughts. Buddhists speak of mindfulness. It is all the same. One Mind. Wakefulness.

Quote, from Sri Nisargadatta Maharaj:
"To know by Being, is Direct Knowledge."

7

Get This Clear

It is already clear. However, you must get it clear in your own mind.

THERE is NO method to AWAKEN.

Wakefulness IS. It is the recognition of this Present wakefulness, which clears the obscuring fixations in the mind.

Wakefulness itself cannot be altered in any way, so all methods and attempts to do so are erroneous, even when they 'appear' to bring some result.

The one who believes in some result that has happened, or will happen, is just a concept also. This will never make sense for the practitioner, since it eliminates the foundation of belief.

Follow the resonance of authenticity in your heart. You may have been following some dead path and have been willing to pay so much for false information that leads nowhere.

In the appearance, all these characters are just phantoms — fictional characters, and this includes the seeker's self-image. All re-presentations of Presence are not Presence — just limited re-presentations of it.

The real teacher is no character. They speak from beyond the facade of 'personalities'. A few 'lucky ones' find a teacher, even though they may appear as ordinary as your next-door neighbor. If you pay attention, you will notice a subtle resonance in Being in yourself, as you respond to contact with him or her.

Quote, from Sri Nisargadatta Maharaj: *"This person (that you believe you are) should be carefully examined and its falseness seen; then its power over you will end."*

8

Confusion

All of your confusion takes form due to one central factor: The view through the mind is seemingly fragmented and conflicting within itself **because pure intelligence has attached itself via the intellect to many beliefs.**

They are all, without exception, simply 'content of mind'. Who you are is centrally placed in this flourishing series of patterns. Direct cognition is pure in everyone without exception. Direct cognition is not 'of' the patterns or the appearances. **Direct Cognition is not personal. It is Universal.**

The false identity that we habitually adhere to, is 'the story of my life'. It will play itself out and no trace will be left. Yet the Universal remains ever Present. THIS space of Knowing is the true identity. **Why sacrifice it for mere beliefs and inner conflict?**

9

Nucleus

You may be new to Non-Duality, or you may have been around it a long time. It really doesn't matter. If you are still searching, it means you have missed the nucleus of the message.

It must strike you with a resonation. This will happen if you open to it. This part is up to you. Some require a devastation to open them up, but it is not necessary.

As a kind of exercise, I suggest you go to the nearest mirror and take a good look at your reflection. Then ask yourself if you really want to be free of seeking? The reflection of yourself will not answer you. You don't expect it to. Yet you expect the mirror in your mind to answer all your requests.

The mind only reflects 'what is'. It interprets what is seen and adds elaborations and distortions to the images. Whatever turns up conceptually in the mind, is not what you are.

Look into the open space, from beyond whatever appears in mind. See through these appearances. Keep looking, until everything is dissolved into transparency. This must continue until it is all done with and your true identity reveals itself.

You will see that what you are is the essence of 'that' which is Seeing.

It needs no conceptual identity and is functioning prior to all concepts. Your true identity is always prior to all concepts and all thoughts. They serve you. Do not attempt to serve them.

This bare or naked Awareness is found to be the essence of freedom itself. You discover, once and for all, that you are indeed already free and that you have been free all along.

It only appears as bondage and belief, and it is only that which seemingly binds you. Apparent limitation only.

What substance does a belief have if you ignore it? Or better still — see through it? The freedom you search for is not going to come from any reflections or additions in mind. It can only be found within your-self as spontaneous, pure Presence — which you already are.

So it is, that we must look into the mirror of the mind and try to find the one that wants freedom. We need to do this as a means of informing the mind of its role.

Then the heart, the core of 'your own' Knowing essence, may send forth a clear message.

10

I Am That

The title above spoken by Sri Nisargadatta Maharaj, conveys a subtle and profound fact for all. Being a 'Jnani', his appearance of 'body-mind' was in India. The word Jnani means, "One who is the 'Formless Knowing Presence'." — Beyond the dualistic realm of mind. He was discovered by a westerner, Maurice Frydman, who organized the recording and transcribing of the contents of the now well-known book, "*I Am That*."

The practices or methods of the (apparent) individual can be seen as a pedagogical means of Self-Knowing Awareness. We could say that all 'experiencing' is equal when viewed in this way.

Direct experiencing is the non-stop activity of Self-Knowing Awareness — no matter 'what' is happening, and no matter 'who' it is 'appearing' to happen to.

Where is the problem? It is all due to conflicting reference points!

A concept of a 'future time', seemingly inhibits the immediate recognition of this instant of Knowing Presence. Whatever problem there appears to be,--investigate the limitations of its mindset. It is all content of mind. Are you that? No! The so-called identified consciousness is just one kind of 'transient' expression in the infinite possibilities of Self-Actualizing Awareness. It is not the actual ever-Present pure nature of Awareness! In the overall scheme of things, what difference can these transient appearances make, in this vast expanse which we call the Universe? Is the seeker just a fiction? A temporary condition?

When all the practices and methods of the seeker have been exhausted, there is no 'hook' left to hang a futuristic 'hope' upon.

The ever-Present, Self-Knowing Awareness is left naked and obvious, un-obscured (to itself). The 'long way home' and the 'short cut' are actually equal.

Since we never depart from this Self-Knowing Awareness, and since the phenomenal conditions are ever changing, it is inevitable that the obvious and unchanging aspect of our own Being reveals its natural expansive freedom. The dis-ease of the 'entity' is transcended in one clean, clear, and open moment of naked Awareness.

With this insight, a natural confidence suffuses our Being-ness. It is found to be the natural and ever-Present fact of Being, beyond all transient conditions.

The mind is pure Knowing.

The concepts that float through the mind are nothing but appearances. Each one appears and each one disappears without a trace. The clear and empty nature of mind remains untouched.

Look and SEE!

You do not have to enter this empty space of Knowing. It already is. It is your own true nature and you have never, ever, left it for one micro-moment or nanosecond.

The 'seeker' will never find it, because the seeker is really nothing but an appearance **in** IT. Even though it appears as something 'other' — there is not one micro-chance that it could have any independent existence, whatsoever.

All the secret knowledge, from all sacred places, amounts to nothing if this innate Knowing is not revealed for the mind. Your direct experiencing of this moment, right now, is the hidden 'prize' that all manner of seekers strive to attain from a position of ignorance. It is an erroneous view!

The ignorance is — the blindness to the obvious fact of, "I am THAT."

As Sri Nisargadatta Maharaj says: *"I am THAT by which I Know I AM"*.

This innate knowledge is embedded in the direct experiencing of every experience. It is Self-Knowing Awareness.

You could not BE without IT.

Quote, from Sri Nisargadatta Maharaj: *"The past is projected into the future and the future betrays you."*

The energy source of all projections by the mind is pure intelligence energy and can only ever arise from this moment of Presence that you ARE. Pay attention and all will be recognised.

11

Do Not Doubt

By consciously occupying this space of Knowing as a gentle effortless alertness, then these habitual tendencies will have less chance to invade and rule the mind.

If you look clearly and directly into the open nature of this moment, you may very well see that there is no uncertainty within the nature of this openness. This thoughtless reality is the ever-present, natural abidance of 'what is'.

While you pay attention to what is presently appearing without fixating on thoughts, the mind will be in abeyance and any thoughts that do arise, will just float through this open space of Knowing.

Everything is found to be clear and obvious. There is no need to trade this open natural clarity for fixating consciousness.

The weight of afflictive emotional life can be left to the past once and for all time. If you do not doubt this possibility, it will unveil its obviousness in Presence and it will do this in a natural way.

Nothing can truly pull or push you out of this endless moment.

You may very well feel an ephemeral solidity of wakefulness that nothing can ever deplete or diminish.

What you see, appears to be painful or joyful in this unfolding. It all takes place, yet there will be an undoubting Presence of mind that remains ever untouched and solid as the age-old rock of truth.

12

Psychological Fixation

What is it that prevents so many from Seeing the message of Non-Duality clearly?

In many who 'approach' this, there is a spiritual smugness, a clever attitude. Quite often the intellect is bright and the mind is quick. You could say it is too quick.

It is this self-centered activity that appears to 'hold ground' and is a belief that 'it' is the Seeing, 'it' is the Knowing. The belief is that 'it' will find the answer, or in some cases 'it' already has the answer.

It certainly may appear to have an answer, but the view is 'mind stuff' and dualistic. It is 'one-up-man-ship'.

Of course, it is all just how it appears in the unfolding of phenomenal life.

Beyond all that, it is so simple and already so.

You can reject all traditions and teachings and go your 'own way' and it will make no difference.

No matter what you 'appear' to 'do', you can never escape one central factor — It is transcended with pure Seeing. Transcending it is in the instant of pure Being, which is Seeing. Transcending it is for the mind only.

The mind's erroneous view is known from beyond its limited view. It is known to be just another appearance in Awareness. Awareness naturally transcends all content of mind. It is even logical, if you want to think it through.

Like pulling focus or 'zooming back' on a telescopic camera lens, the open view instantly includes all other views 'before' it — without any obscuration or distortion.

Like removing 'the filters of the mind', Seeing is freed from the apparent limited distortions of the dualistic mind and habitual fixations. 'Seeing' itself is always free of these limitations.

The elusive and commonly overlooked central factor is that there is a belief in being a 'person'.

The 'person' is a psychological fixation. A fixation with being a mind in a body. Both body and mind are 'mine'. It is a belief in being something solid and real. This belief is appearing with and 'as' a habitual image — self-image. It is a belief in being a permanent fixture.

Seeing is Knowing. Knowing is Seeing. This spontaneous Seeing-Knowing is pure functioning — prior to all beliefs and mind processes. **'Belief' is in 'time'. In other words, it takes time for a belief to unfold in the mind.** It is basically a story. A process.

Seeing-Knowing, are One in pure functioning and are spontaneous — instant. Forever instant. Don't skip over this fact. See it. Nothing can alter this fact. Everything is spontaneously appearing — all is arising 'equally' from the One source in this Singular Instant. The First and only Instant. Seeing this fact, is not an intellectual process. In other words, no deviation in mind takes place in direct cognition.

'Time' is mind and mind is time. A deviation from this moment, this Presence, is in 'mind process' only.

Time and space patterns all hang off the self-centre. There is no coming or going in this first instant of direct cognition. The one that believes that it leaves this and comes back is what is called the 'person' — the psyche.

All psychological suffering is hinged on this belief in being a 'person'.

No matter how distasteful this 'pointing' may

appear to be for the personality — there is no escape from this cycle unless this fixation is transcended.

How do we do this? How do we transcend this belief? In the delineation of appearing to be a 'person', it excludes all open concepts of boundless Awareness. The personal cannot be the impersonal. The impersonal appears as the 'personal' without changing in essence. It is all already happening in its completeness.

'Your' belief in being a 'person' (with all its baggage) is just an obstacle to this clear open view of immediate Knowing. This natural Knowing is beyond all belief without exception.

It is all in Seeing. Simply see what is clearly obvious. It is NOT an Object!

Realize that this common erroneous belief is actually transparent. There is Seeing of this immediately — in this instant.

Pure Seeing is cutting through all transparent belief right now. **Drop the concept that you are a 'person' and simply be the Seeing.**

In this open view, where is the belief? How obvious it all is. Yet no 'person' can ever see it.

Is there still a question of why this is so?

It is because the pure functioning of Seeing, which is pure Knowing, is not a psychological process. **How can a concept see?** It is obvious that it will never be the pure function of Seeing. Seeing is Knowing. Seeing and Knowing are One.

This pure functioning does not depend on any subsidiary process of mind. All conditioning is acquired in 'time'. It unfolds in 'time'.

The mystery for mind, which is time, is that there is only now. The psychological 'person' depends on 'time', for without it, it cannot appear. Let it appear — know it for what it is.

Can you find any substantial, simple evidence, in direct cognition of this elusive 'time' without adding more thoughts to it?

In looking for it, simply notice that this looking is only ever happening now. You cannot look from a yesterday or a tomorrow. Neither can you look from a moment ago or from a moment in the future.

This revelation is a profound yet simple and ordinary fact of Being. It is truly already Known in this innate Knowing — this intelligence that you are.

There is a Zen saying: "Before Enlightenment, chop wood, carry water. After Enlightenment, chop wood, carry water." I would put it this way: Forget about Enlightenment! There is only ever 'chopping wood' (the immediacy). No before or after. In other words, all there is, is activities appearing upon this spontaneous cognition, this spontaneous Seeing - Knowing - Being. Everything, including apparent 'doing', appears upon this naked cognition.

Everything is happening spontaneously, yet nothing really happens. When you truly understand this, there is no 'you', no 'person' there that understands it at all. Nothing to claim and no one to claim anything.

There is an un-doubt-able immediate Knowing — all contained in pure Seeing. There is only understanding and this is nothing other than direct cognition - Seeing - Knowing, shining through the mind.

Quotes, from Sri Nisargadatta Maharaj: *"Your difficulty lies in wanting reality and being afraid of it at the same time. You are afraid of it because you do not know it. To know reality is to be in harmony with it. In harmony there is no place for fear."*
"You cannot destroy the false, for you are creating it all the time. Withdraw from it, ignore it, go beyond and it will cease to be."

13

The Paradox

The paradox is only for the identified, partial, personalized consciousness.

One aspect of it is this: All beliefs, without exception, whether they are the beliefs of a fool or those of a brilliant philosopher — they are all just appearances in 'time'. All corroborating evidence, which appears to support these manifold beliefs, is also time bound in a 'realm of mind' only.

The actuality is always this Presence, right now, it is non-conceptual, thoughtless reality.

The essential nature of all things is Silently Present, as this immediate vast unlimited Presence. It is your true nature and like the true nature of mind, it is clear and empty — yet full of Knowing.

All of this universal material appearance is floating, suspended in a vast endless, timeless space of Knowing - Awareness. It is this Knowing Presence, which is so familiar to you — yet you have continually missed its significance. This un-mediated Knowing, is ever available because it IS timeless Presence.

Its essence can never be reduced to an objectified 'thing' in mind (or outside of the mind). Even so, the mind appears to do this constantly.

Nothing compounds into anything in this timeless open space of Knowing. The intellect is seemingly frustrated by this, and as it tries (appears as a trying) to approach the immediate empty nature of mind, recognition arises that 'it' indeed is not that which is Knowing.

A moment of humbleness may happen for the ego as its foundations vanish.

The essential simplicity of Being, is this immediate Presence - Being - Knowing.

It is this Presence — right now. There is nothing you need to 'do' in respect of this.
It just IS. Be warm and open to it — that is all.

It is yourself.

14

Innately Present

Question: "It is hard to know if I am really communicating this clearly or not since there is obviously some confusion going on here. I guess some of it may boil down to the "understanding" seemingly being restricted to the intellect at times — like, "Well, I can see that point, and it brings some relief, yet I can't take it wholeheartedly because there is still some worry or fear happening" — and it appears to be "deeper" at other times — which really can't be explained in words.

Gilbert: Stand in the bathroom, in front of the mirror. The attention slides from what you are to an image of self (body), the image in the mirror. You can't see yourself in the way that you can see your reflection. (Speaking in the terms of the body, etc.)

Without getting into the vanity aspect of it all, the image appears to be alive. Where is the immediate livingness? There is a lot of self-referencing going on. The image may appear to take on a 'life' of its own. Keep in mind that this is only an analogy. Don't construct new beliefs from this. Just see and know. Understand clearly. Misunderstanding is conflicting concepts, while Pure Seeing is non- conceptual. If the image in the mirror speaks to you, you will jump out of your skin and run for the doorway. The image can't do anything. We believe in a multitude of images of the self and we believe in the projected images of, 'others'-'outside'.

There is an ancient story of King Solomon. He takes on the appearance of a beggar in his own Kingdom and enters self-exile for twenty years. Without the burden of an image of being a King, he experiences firsthand, the ordinary 'life and times' of his people, with none of the privileges belonging to his habitual 'self-image'. In this way he gains new insights, with which he can rule his Kingdom with compassion and wisdom. These qualities are not gained because they are innately present in us all. They are ONE and not separate in any way.

The extended 'story' mentioned is full of symbolism pertaining to our true essence and the falsehood of mere images.

Note: We use the word Self only as a means to discuss something that is not an object. The true Self is our authenticity while the represented image is apt to be so easily false, biased and eccentric.

To see the True, we need 'to Be the True'. In going beyond the limits of fear, especially those about our self, we find our true freedom, which was always Present.

Fear? What is it? Without labeling it with 'past' interpretations, let it be. Know it thoroughly and it will appear to transform itself. It will reveal its nature. Be warm towards it, have a love towards this Self and do the investigation. If we have a purpose, then it can only be that. See and know that 'Seeing' is always from the primary 'space-like Awareness'.

It is not a 'person'. In Belief, it appears as an image of a person.

Are you truly that? Isn't it an appearance in mind?

Belief is a terrain of agreement and disagreement in 'common mind' only. It is not the direct evidence of simple Presence. There is no problem in this, but if the energy of belief shifts via identification into an image, then MAYA appears to take over and so it appears to have 'got you'. That is 'her' job.

All this can tend to feel a little dramatic — it is the drama of life. In essence it is so simple, but in detail, so complicated.

Be the essence of it all.

It is what you are anyway. Being. This natural Presence. Presence to the appearances which arise in Seeing — in Knowing.

Stop beating yourself up. Let the movie film roll on — as it does whether you want it or not.

Love, play, act, as if you are in the play but know full well it is all just appearing. Enter consciously into the role of the apparent puppet — with loving Presence, free of judgment.

Whatever is happening is the work of intelligence energy. Feel the sensations in the right arm. The left arm sensations appear also (in this same place.) The whole body is there. It is this immediate livingness. There is a subtle Presence which we may have ignored for 'too long'.

This moment opens up, revealing that there is no time at all, apart from THIS moment.

Let conscious Awareness spread to all the body and beyond, the floor, the room, the house, the street, the extended terrain, the globe, the space. It is not imaginary.

The imagery that pops up is not of the direct sensation or direct Knowing. Knowing is beyond all content of mind.

The actuality is real in the immediacy. One full moment of conscious Awareness is all it takes.

One kiss from eternal Presence.

You see that it is already happening endlessly. It has always been so.

It is this immediate Presence — the livingness of conscious life. What is the nature of those troublesome unconscious beliefs? Find out what you are and in so doing you find out that you are not those 'things' that 'come and go'.

What is the nature of the limitations we place on our being Presence?

Contemplate this.

15

Coercion

Is it possible that you have been unwittingly coerced into a state of feeling isolated and separate from a sense of wholeness? Is it true? Who is that? Is that what you are?

Have you lost a natural love for yourself because of 'others'? You are present and aware right now. See and know from the source that you are, Awareness, AS THIS moment.

It appears as a 're-claiming' of your natural state, which is full of warmth and love. When this warmth is nurtured, it spreads out and touches everything in body, mind and beyond. A natural radiance of Presence, yet having no location.

It is truly your natural inherent stateless state, which appears to have been temporarily covered over by concepts and habitual states of belief, self-protection, reaction and inattention.

This re-claiming is not by thought. Believing in secondhand and contrived thoughts is one of the main culprits. Clarity is ever present.

The natural state is already present, just

covered over by divergent fixations in mind. Projected concepts and images. Look NOW. Is this true in this immediacy? Seeing.

The natural state is beyond the limits of forgetting and remembering. Pay attention to your immediate life in this moment. Be attentive and open to 'what is'.

Even if some drama arises, it will last a certain 'time' and it will pass. If you let it be just as it is, without attaching your identity to it in any way and in not dwelling on its associative reverberations, then it will fall away or pass by without incident. We don't have to carry it around with us.

16

No Owner

The only obstacle to a complete open view is a habitual fixation within the intellect.

It appears to be a stubborn stumbling block for so many. However, when the basis of this fixation reveals its insubstantial nature, even the most stubborn intellect is rendered passive. The energy of belief ceases to support the erroneous evidence. Pure Seeing is completely free and spontaneously happening right now.

The intellect follows as close as it can but it is a borrower only. It takes on fixated forms in mind and that includes the belief that 'it' is Seeing, that 'it' is Knowing. This is a complete fabrication yet this fact will never be accepted by the intellect willingly. It wants proof, yet it ignores the clear and obvious. The pure functions are not owned by any 'entity'.

False ownership will dissolve if it is challenged by a conscious investigation.

Fixations in mind do not belong to your authenticity — natural Being.

The psychological 'you' will never embrace it while a belief of separation continues. When you cease to project an 'image' of a false self, it will appear that your true essence embraces and enfolds everything into this Pure Presence that you ARE.

This dissolution may overwhelm the organism and a sense of humility and relief may spread as an immediate response throughout your Being. You are not the response. You are the direct cognition only.

This humility is a temporary condition and will dissolve into simple Presence as long as the mind does not grasp for a familiar habitual condition or some sentimentality (a state of mind).

Be warm towards yourself and let your love of Presence remain free.

If there is a strong habitual pattern of inflexible perception, this hold of the intellect may require many strikes from many angles with forceful shocks to shift its eccentric stubborn stance in mind.

These habits are somewhat like crystallizations or states. (Remember that they have no real substance.) As things loosen up, impressions are not translated in the habitual way and one gets a taste of this ever-fresh nature of simple Presence.

Then the old identified point of reference called the self-center is dissolved or is at least in abeyance with this true 'prior to all' intelligence. Fresh insights bring a new impulse for openness and to remain open. Watching (Seeing) from this relaxed openness, one will notice the habitual conditions from spaciousness without fixating on them.

They may appear to try and reassert themselves, yet they have no power as long as you remain alert. Eventually they will appear to give themselves up and cease to invade your natural Presence.

This is the 'age old' realm of Self-Knowledge. This singular and immediate moment, of Self-Knowledge — Self-Knowing — is real.

It is THIS moment of SELF-Knowing Awareness. It is only THIS immediacy. It is not in some 'other time', than THIS moment. It is obvious that 'This moment' is all there IS.

It is not somewhere else. No practice is needed.

This is not contestable or negotiable.

You are THAT.

17

Right Here

Right here, right now, the Ultimate reality is clearly obvious. Yet no one sees it as obvious. People imagine that they will come 'into' an Ultimate Understanding. This is an impossibility.

The fabrication of a 'person' has no bearing on the ever-present Universal Essence of Being, which is the understanding itself. The 'person' is a concept that only 'appears to be'.

As the 'personal' fades into empty space, which happens many times a day for all of us, the clear, direct and immediate cognizance is left, as it is, with no encumbrances — As it always IS.

The mind caught in seeking, misses the obvious. This immediacy is so obvious and so clearly evident — yet few see its true value.

As an individualized pattern of energy, you are submerged in it like a whale in the ocean. There are no words that can describe it because it is beyond all description and language. It is not a state! Yet it is so profoundly Present. Every particle in this universe is suspended in this vast un-mediated Presence.

Without naming anything, without creating a conceptual world of particles, all is seen to be transparent, empty. The vastness in front of your eyes, and the vastness behind your eyes, is One singular vast Presence.

Everything that appears, appears to float within your own space of Knowing — your 'true nature'. Always immediate, it is this immediate living-ness.

The obvious and clear evidence appears to be obscured, simply because the content of mind is believed to be something substantial.

Wakefulness is never obscured. Its very nature is open intelligence — unconditioned by any past. There is not even a speck of dust (objectivity) in this clear and open cognizance.

The 'entity' is simply a conceptual appearance in THIS. Paradoxically for the dualistic mind, there is no one that can know this.

Knowing IS. Knowing is prior to every-thing, including all identities or personalities. No matter 'who' you are, no matter 'where' you are, the basic situation is the same for all of us.

Right there, there is a body appearing in space. It is nothing other than the immediate expression of this immediate intelligence, energy appearing as a form.

Within this (your) body there also appears (most probably) a habitual concept regarding an 'individual', an 'entity' that resides in this body.

"Yes, it is me," you may say. In the 'space of Knowing', in which everything appears, this concept of a 'me' also appears.

If one looks into, investigates this appearance of a 'me', (this concept or idea) it reveals something extraordinary, distinctly different from the usual apparent view of the so-called, individual.

All objects appear in this OPEN space of Knowing and nowhere else. If you do not consciously include this (your) body and the content of mind within this space of Knowing, then the apparent substantiality of an 'entity' (me) is not transcended.

For the so-called, seeker of truth, in the story of its search, this minor step or movement of attention can be a major turning point. Without a thought and without relying on any mind processing or naming, something quite extraordinary opens up. We can call it a shift in perspective. However, this open perspective has always been here.

Drop all ideas about time, past, present and future and sit with this immediacy. Without a thought or concept it is all clear, open, spontaneous living.

Obvious pure clarity in Being. It is too subtle for the word based mind, because in its entire, wondrous, boundless expanse, it is utterly non-conceptual.

The First Instant of cognition is non-conceptual. This first instant is ever present. One Moment of Eternal Realization.

All that you actually see is this immediate living-ness. The acquired mind of learned 'things' adds its words and concepts. These appear within the scope of pure Seeing, so you can deduct from that, that Seeing is prior to words and concepts.

All concepts and appearances are appearing within the scope of Seeing. How can an appearance appear without Seeing? What you truly are in this moment is cognizing emptiness, it is actually 'non-Being', from which ALL Being-ness arises.

You cannot know this in any fixed and finite way because it is infinite and ever fresh.

Pure Knowing is it, yet this is never a 'thing' in

a 'world'. All worlds appear in this Infinite Knowing. There is no entity in this to be concerned or not concerned and that will always appear as a paradox for the intellect. However, when the foundations of erroneous belief loosen there may arise an apparent increase in resonance with this infinite Knowing. It remains as pure Knowing, and words fail to express it. The sharing of such Knowing as knowledge is not possible because it is always prior to any conceptual, verbal bridge that may be apparently constructed by teacher and his/her pupil.

Clearing out erroneous beliefs, reveals what is Already Present. The basic fact of immediate 'Being' is the first instant of Knowing.

It is what you are and it is always direct and immediate experiencing no matter how it appears in its phenomenal aspect.

What are doubts made of?

Contemplate this.

18

Knowing

'Who' is it that is looking for the absolute truth? It is right here, in front of your eyes. It is right here behind your eyes.

It is One Wholeness.

The imaginary boundary between, 'in front' and 'behind', is empty of any substance. No 'entity' resides there or anywhere else. Knowing that is freedom.

All there is, is Knowing.

You, are that immediate Knowing. Right now! There is actually no possibility in THIS authentic Presence when or where you could not be THIS Knowing.

In Seeing that this is what I am, then all the mental anguish ceases and all the turbulence subsides and everything is known to be clear and obvious. And yet it IS always so.

Love yourself and let this Knowing blossom into its natural wordless reality — of simple wakefulness.

There is no harm done anywhere, despite your belief that there may be harm done somewhere. See that it is all of 'somewhere else' and in 'some other time'. The dissolution and the resurrection is appearing and disappearing in THIS moment. It is appearance only. Like a rainbow, you cannot prove that a rainbow ever existed as anything with substance.

This moment, is all there is — it is One Eternal Moment — One Instant.

This, is immediate life. I call it the First Instant. You have never left THIS, not even for a fraction of time.

THIS very moment, is the unbound vastness of the ever-present NOW. You, are this pure duration, which is endless.

Where is the doubt?

19

Reality

Presence, Presence. Just — Presence.

You are present and aware. 'Feel into' this Presence that you are. Do not imagine anything, just feel into it. Let the senses be open.

Presence. It is not an object, yet it contains all apparent objects. It is not a subject, yet it contains all apparent subjects. It has no specific qualities, yet it contains all qualities equally.

Simple Presence. The Ultimate Reality is That which spontaneously knows that it, is. It is thoughtless, yet it contains all thought. It is not imaginary, yet it contains all imagination.

Presence. "**I am Presence and nothing other than That.**"

20

Bird in Flight

Watch a bird in flight. All there is, is this immediacy. You cannot predict its pathway accurately.

The bird glides through space and nothing attaches to this spontaneous movement. No dots mark the sky with its flight path.

The past does not appear in its immediate flight. The future remains unknown. All you ever see is this immediacy. It is life.

This is the direct and immediate situation at all times, whether you believe that you see it or not. If 'you' are caught up in mind stuff, then the dualistic mind is occupied with fixations, and the spontaneous Non-Dual nature of all things is missed.

See directly for yourself whether what I am saying is true or not. In not making this investigation, then all these words or indicators remain useless. Just words.

Let's look at this again in a slightly different

way: What possible benefit is there in continuing with these limited, fluctuating and time bound view of being separate and alone?

The imaginary path of a seeker is scattered with obstacles, suffering and all manner of afflicted emotions. The bliss of completion is always conceptually placed, 'just over the hill'. Open your eyes and see. See from an un-contrived natural state of Presence, which is here behind or beyond the transient states of mind.

In your search for meaning, you attempt to see this ultimate reality, and because it is everywhere and because it is everything, you cannot say that you cannot see it.

Immediate Knowing is IT — IT is Seeing!

What this means is that this activity of Knowing happening with you right now, is the very same foundation, the very same essence that is found everywhere in the vast array - this dynamic display of Presence Awareness. No separation exists.

How can you say that you do not know THIS? How could you be without THIS? **All thoughts, emotions, images, objects and all mind realms appear in THIS.**

Observe the fact that they also disappear in THIS. Without the slightest deviation from THIS all-inclusive Presence. Recognize that you ARE as you have always been — Present and Aware. You are inseparable from THIS ISNESS.

No boundary — anywhere!

Supremely ordinary and obvious, clear as the space immediately in front of you.

With no process at all, and with no imaginary division, it remains open as it always IS. Who can divide the indivisible?

Who can change the unchanging?

Come back to the ever-fresh eternal moment of Being-ness.

Live from THAT.

With insight and time, it does appear to consolidate into a constant Knowing, yet the essence is always clear and empty. Timelessly Present.

Such Knowing reveals itself in the Spacious, non-fixating Awareness. Because that is, what it is. In this, there is an absence of anything like a 'someone seeking something'.

The story ceases - if only for a moment. The essence of this Knowing is not accumulating into any form of knowledge.

In the First Instant — Pure Intelligence IS Knowing!

IT also 'appears' as everything. Knowing is ever prior to anything known. The 'known' comes and goes while Knowing remains.

This fact will always appear paradoxical for the dualistic mind of a seeker — even though such a mind has no substance at all in itself.

Who would believe it? It is a story for the mind! It is nothing but a story. So, full stop.

One moment — One Presence — One Knowing.

If you look closely at what is happening with regard to thinking, you will see that thoughts appear quite spontaneously.

The thinker is an addition and really is only another thought.

The long standing habituated attitude or belief is that: "I am thinking," or "They are my thoughts," and "I believe such and such." "This is my accumulated knowledge," etc. All this is related to a self-centered reference point, which we call 'me'. With a little looking or the simplicity of just watching what is actually happening, you will see that thoughts simply appear and disappear. Do they leave any trace? Without claiming them as 'mine', they just dissolve spontaneously.

This is not a method of ridding oneself of thoughts or that thoughts are bad. It is simply to come to see what they are — they are all in 'the realm of appearances'.

Without feeding them with the energy of belief, they simply disappear.

All of this may, of course, be a direct challenge to the self-centre. There may appear a strong resistance which could be said to be a struggle for the survival of a belief system. However, it is just more of the same content of mind in partnership with a conceptually based, emotional reaction, to an imagined threat. All this hangs off other reference points — of a 'me' and 'other than me' — conflicting thoughts. Separation!

NOW, realize THIS: Separation is only a concept! It is an old story that supports the belief in being a separate 'entity' with territories called, 'Mine' and 'Not Mine'. It is just nonsense, and it is easily seen through with a little open investigation.

In the simplicity of looking, in Seeing clearly what is actually taking place, we begin to discriminate the erroneous from the actual. This is all that is needed.

You, are present and aware in this first instant. This is the actuality, right now. It cannot be otherwise. Without moving away conceptually from this simplicity, see that all is clear and obvious in this Seeing from this actual and immediate functioning — this simple wakefulness.

Quote, from Sri Nisargadatta Maharaj: *"You will understand neither the body nor consciousness unless you go beyond both."*

21

Who Knows?

Knowing, is consistently and immediately here without any process of mind needed for its continuous flow. It is indeed, spontaneous Knowing.

No practice can create Knowing. No method can really alter this immediate Knowing — livingness — because the livingness is the source of all, including any apparent method.

The method is always secondary and never touches the essence of Presence Awareness.

It is unlimited intelligence, in all its immediacy.

Who doubts this? Only the limited and biased intellect of a 'me'. It is only in the appearance, and as an appearance, any benefit, merit, success, or failure, can appear and disappear in this Knowing Presence. The 'entity' that is a belief in being worthy or unworthy is born of mind and is totally transient.

The mind is clear and empty.

No bondage is present if one really opens the mind and looks into it.

Direct cognition reveals all, just as it is.

Bring your attention to this immediate fact and see for yourself. Awareness is an aspect of the singular constant. Awareness is the Seeing. Awareness is the Knowing. Unbound, Pure Consciousness — Pure Awareness.

It is pure immediate Being. It is not an entity! It is NOT somewhere else! This, is it, right now. It is pure cognizing. It is Self-Knowing Awareness. All is a never ending unfolding of appearance — within this unchanging Omniscient Being.

The Absolute 'Presence of Knowing' penetrates all 'things', including all teachers, Gurus, ordinary beings, all methods and practices in this apparent endless pedagogical journey. It is Self-Knowing Awareness in all its diversity.

The drunk on the corner, the girl on the till at the supermarket, the dodgy car salesman, the bus driver, the guy you dislike the most, the ex-wife, the ex-husband, the pleasant priest, the selfish priest, they all have their place in the scheme of 'things'. They too, are nothing but appearances within Omniscient Being. One Taste - One Essence of Being.

22

Light

When all words cease, the natural Being is left naked and complete in its harmonious state of clear openness.

Without a thought, there is nothing you can say about it. It is neither right nor wrong — it just IS.

Some 'seekers' express a need for a method, a method for holding onto whatever it is that they value in their personalized estimations. The 'seeker' only appears to dominate consciousness with its needs.

Words, words, words — everyone wants a method to practice for this elusive Self-Realization, which is only imagined.

Denial (ignorance) of the 'Ever Present Evidence' of complete Freedom, is the apparent bondage. The true teacher will not give any false hope and so they relentlessly reveal to you the uselessness of methods. In the same moment, your own innate freedom is revealed as a direct communication in and as the immediacy of freedom itself.

Communication of pure intelligence with itself;
It is ONE.

This essence lies behind the facade of 'the personal'.

Through exhaustion, dismantling, or by a 'blow' from freedom itself, the 'seeker' comes to its end.

The 'now' is then known to be free of all constructions of mind including all methods and purifying practices. It is already pure Being.

There are NO Non-Dual practices or methods. When you open your eyes in the morning, do you have to use some method, or make a practice of this simple wakefulness? Isn't it already here at all times? This simple wakefulness is Non-Dual Awareness.

No practice or concept is needed at all. It can never be a practice! All these methods can only appear to lead you back to the essence of this — THIS Non-Dual moment.

And, so it is, that the 'journey' of Self-discovery is simply a long or short pedagogical journey in 'time', psychology, and relativity.

It is all Self-Knowing Awareness — no matter 'how' or 'what' it appears as. Nothing is really right or wrong in this apparent journey into Realization. It is all actualized as it is.

There are no exceptions in this. You are present and aware right now. There is no other 'time'. This is always the case. You cannot get out of this 'now'. You have never been anywhere but right here in this 'now' — because THIS, is all there IS and ever IS.

So, since you are already Present and Aware, whatever you discover is both yourself and not yourself.

In the appearance, it is all 'in' duality — in essence, it is Non-Dual. There is an appearance of consciousness re-discovering itself over and over, moment by moment in this apparent journey. In this appearance of a separate individual, what you truly are is revealed, once and for all time.

Even though it may appear as a repeating revelation, your natural essence is ever prior to the pedagogical journey.

You are! — before, during and after all apparent journeys.

In essence you do not actually move from this immediacy, this fact of Being. Thinking arises in Being. A fixation happens and an apparent 'entity' is born in mind. It is a transient appearance — without any independent being or power. It is a mirage.

Innately you know this.

Being – Seeing – Knowing. It is light — and light is love. You love to be — and you ARE. What 'more' is there? There are appearing endless journeys in this vast Being-ness. When all the journeys are over, Being remains as it always IS.

Quote, from Sri Nisargadatta Maharaj: *"Keep quiet and watch what comes to the surface of the mind"*

23

Freedom Flows

It is so direct that the apparent bridge between what you are, and what you seek, dissolves as the teaching is revealed to be nothing other than THIS immediate actuality of Being Presence — THIS Immediate Knowing.

There is NO such thing as a Non-Dual Teaching. There is NO such thing as a Non-Dual Teacher. All experiencing is nothing but the pedagogical means of Self-Knowing Awareness — without exceptions (for the mind).

All 'experiences' of the so-called 'past' are 'apparent' deviations in mind only, if they are fixated on. The singular essence of these deviations is actually immediate experiencing, as they arise. When do they arise otherwise? They can only appear in THIS immediate moment, now.

Once this is known fully, then freedom flows as the spontaneous living-ness. Paradoxically for the mind, this is actually always the case - in this immediate moment of actualized Awareness.

There is Knowing and this can only be in and as this Presence we commonly call 'Now'.

The question is: 'Who' can't see this? And indeed 'who' can see it? When this 'who' is seen through (disengaged) consciously, via the potency of direct cognition, then the apparent separation is no more. It is known to have never been.

There is only Knowing. There is no independent 'person' Knowing anything at all. As long as there is belief in a 'someone who knows' then there is conceptual bondage — but that is only 'in the appearance' and not in 'the actual' immediate life.

Quote, from Sri Nisargadatta Maharaj: *"Understanding is all."*

The subtleties of that quotation are beyond all concepts.

Seeing-Knowing is happening — Period.

24

A Fresh Clearing

Could it be possible that all problems, which appear in the mind, are so-called problems simply due to conflicting conceptual forms or erroneous mind interpretations, which appear only in the mind itself?

It appears that circumstances compound into a series of complex representations in the 'mind realm' of 'time'.

The past and future appear to loom over us, yet they are simple concepts supported (as being something actual) only by belief. No one knows what will happen. It all unfolds without cause or reason. That is a challenge for the intellect. 'Who' is challenged? If you were told that none of these problems are actually true, it may be quite difficult to accept such news to be correct or true. Who could possibly believe in such a revelation? No one! (No one in their 'right mind'?) The ever-present pure-functioning of 'direct cognition' is directly Present as this 'actuality', in all its immediacy in every moment — and furthermore, it is this 'immediacy' itself, which cuts through 'all time realms' without exception.

It does this simply because it is immediate — un-mediated Knowing.

Nothing actually compounds into anything that can be held to be separate and/or independent from 'this immediacy' — this 'living now'.

All conceptual postulations about this (or about anything at all) can only ever 'appear' in this now (this Presence) and they are either seen to be conceptual or they are believed to be substantial — and so they seemingly consume the attention in 'the realm of extensions in time and belief'.

In simply paying attention to what is actually directly happening, the mind is spontaneously brought back to this immediacy — its own pure functioning.

Everything is seen to be appearing before or within one's (unlimited) Presence without entering into any extension in so-called 'time'.

Whatever forms as a concept or as an 'object of knowledge' -- that form will disappear.

In the immediacy of our attention (Awareness) there is witness-ing of concepts appearing and disappearing. This direct and profound revelation appears as an opening of the mind into a fresh view, which is 'then' found to be ceaselessly Present.

This fresh view is not something new like a 'new presentation'. Even though this open view has been here all along, it appears, for the mind, to be a fresh clearing. Beliefs dissolve and in vanishing from view or simply disappearing – it leaves a sense of more space. The habit is for the mind to grasp at this and 'create' a new realm of delusion. In essence it is actually not some newly acquired state of affairs. It 'was' and is happening always, yet nothing compounds into any 'thing' with separateness.

Knowing is happening. This is tasted as unmediated Presence - directly, not as a conceptual possibility but as the everpresent actuality — the nature of Awareness itself.

The true nature of mind is clear and empty. All systems of knowledge fail in ascertaining such directness because they themselves are not direct and are always based on concepts. These concepts of the past occupy the mind and so directness is seemingly subjugated or missed via identification.

One must ask: 'who' misses the obvious? It is already here as the very nature of (your own) Awareness.

Intelligence suffuses all systems and they are all ancillary. With applied intelligence, through the alignment of the intellect with 'the actual', everything falls into place. With intellectual resistance, inner conflict or complaint, the functioning feels bogged down and Awareness appears to be obscured from its open and clear Presence. This obscuration only happens for the fixating mind content, which includes a long-standing identification with being a separate entity which believes that 'it knows' something.

'Who' can't see this? Seeing is happening! Paradoxically for the intellect, this Seeing is not actually compounding into any substance, knowledge, or any concept, about what is 'seen' or even 'what' is doing the Seeing.

Seeing is simply happening! The 'seer' and the 'seen' are like two ends to 'the stick of Seeing'.

Investigating directly, whatever appears as 'thought', and the 'library of self-knowledge' or the 'known', quite naturally brings to the fore, 'direct Knowing', which has always been present, yet seemingly overlooked.

The 'clearing' reveals the true clarity of mind. Once truly tasted, it shows itself 'more and more', in a manner of speaking.

Direct Knowing is prior to 'the known'. It cuts through the known and reveals the 'foundations' of belief.

You are free.

You have always been free. Why sacrifice this freedom for mere transitory states, thoughts and 'beliefs'? They all disappear when they are really looked into.

Investigate what has been indicated and see for yourself.

25

Nothing Else

This is a message, don't get caught up with the messenger.

Stick to the essence of the message: "I am, as you are, the source of the message, the message, the messenger and the receiver of the message."

Once received, it is no longer necessary.

'What' is it that you are afraid of? Contemplate on that for a moment, without getting lost in it, without the slightest exaggeration:

"In this moment of right now, I sit here in the subtle Presence of freedom."

This freedom is yours also:

"All the past is rendered into a passive memory that has no power over me. The future is of no concern to me at all. I AM."

I am telling something so simple. It is a legacy, a natural birthright. In 'the appearance', this legacy was given to me. (Uncovered)

In 'the appearance', it offers itself to you in each moment. It belongs to you. You have only *seemingly* lost it. In this 'now' there is an opening, a space of natural freedom.

What is it that you are afraid of? You have been told so often of — and about, this freedom. It is not somewhere else. Life itself nudges you continuously with its immediate touch.

How many ways must you be told — before your mind steps beyond its conceptual bondage?

You are FREE, right NOW.

If you follow the following suggestions, you will see this:

Let the restless winds of the mind subside.
Let all doubts dissolve into open space.
Do not grasp at anything.
Let the mind rest on nothing at all.
Let it float into its natural spaciousness.
Everything IS.
It is clear and obvious.
THIS is IT—this actuality of potent Presence of Being.
You ARE Present and Aware.
Your essential true nature is equal to (and with) all that you see — as it always has been.
Do not wait for anything else.
There is nothing else.

The train of compulsion 'stops' HERE.
Imaginary 'journeys' 'out' of THIS 'now', can
only 'appear' to take you away from THIS
IS-ness.

You ARE present and aware.
It is ALL you need and have.
Let your doubts vanish into this IS-ness.
It is final.

THIS - IS - IT

Quote, from Sri Nisargadatta Maharaj: *"You know everything but you do not know yourself, for the Self is not known through words. Only direct insight will reveal it"*

26

Gods and Gurus

If you're wandering about in the guise of a seeker, then you have created a series of gods in your mind. One god is your own self-image. Another may be a guru or teacher 'out there' somewhere. Money, food, sex have all taken on god-like forms for most.

You may want 'it' to come and save you from your other inner gods and vanquish or dissolve confusion and dis-ease. The sad revelation is that He, She, or It, will never come and save you. How can a fabricated image save you? Save you from what? Your own imagination?

It is in our dreams that we have created a heaven and hell. It is relative and limited. Heaven and Hell are the polar opposites of the dualistic mind. Angelic thoughts and demonic thoughts play off each other in a confused mind.

The kingdom of freedom is (hidden) within your own heart essence. Presence has no boundary. Its influence is 'finding' its way to you in many ways if you pay attention.

The use of less biased dualistic concepts is

only to assist the mind in being free of habits of bondage. It's another paradox! Find the first instant of conscious Being-Awareness. It IS what you are. The one who finds it, is THAT. Merge with that and see from that 'place'.

Everything is clear and obvious. There are no gods or entities anywhere.

Your view is pristinely open and obvious. Back in the place from which Seeing is happening, there is a clear open space. Be that.

Why do you invite all those imaginary gods and images, with their conflicting natures, into this open view?

The peace beyond all understanding is non-conceptual Awareness. Concepts appear to take over simply because we do not fully occupy this space of Knowing Presence, AS SIMPLE WAKEFULNESS.

As a conceptual being, it cannot be done. As the actual, it does not need to be done, because it already is.

27

Ever Present

Even though (in the ultimate view) there is no transmission, here in the world of seekers and gurus, it does appear that there is.

Only from open Awakened Awareness, is the riddle resolved. From the perspective of a 'seeker' it appears that a transmission is necessary and desirable.

Original Seeing is undivided and does not have any qualities of being a finite point, because it contains all points as such and is the very vastness of Presence Awareness, (which is timeless and unbounded.)

Even so, it does appear that one who is free in this life can assist to bring another into the same open view. The one who is free, knows full well that the 'other' is already 'there' (so to speak), and the introduction is simply a vibrational connection held long enough for the 'other' to taste this freedom, fully in themselves. Then it's over! The full deliverance into open Awareness appears to take 'time'. In this duration-less, 'pure duration', THIS moment, you have never been lost.

This belief in conceptualised time and process is a false sense of reality and has no security.

Once this 'new view' of open Awareness stabilises, it is noticed that there is no interest in the 'old' view and 'before', (memory) contain nothing that is necessary or needed.

Presence is full and washes over all content and the fragmentation of previous views, disappear into its origin — impartiality. The barest factual memories are still available, but are known to be nothing but spontaneous patterns of energy or a reflection in the stillness of mind. They are nothing but Presence (seemingly gone) and have no independent nature of themselves. They no longer trigger off states of wanting or desire for more of anything with which they are associated.

It all simply IS as it is.

All the fuss and bother about Enlightenment is known to be completely unnecessary. The dramatic search for Enlightenment is a joke. The one who can truly see that, is beyond the humor or sadness of this joke and beyond the drama of a search 'out there'.

So much has been written on Non-Duality, some of it is clear, but most of it is just messy dualistic notions disguised in fancy Non-Dual language.

To the one who is free, this is of no consequence or concern. Who cares? The 'person' is an appearance. When that is fully known, then all the patterns which appear, (along with the apparent 'person'), are simply a play of energy and do not compound into anything at all.

Space-like Awareness remains free of all content.

There is no entity, nor any 'doer', apart from an appearance in mind. How many appearances have appeared? It is ceaseless.

In looking from the space in which Seeing is happening, all is clear and empty.

It is seen that there is no substantial foundation for any stance to be taken, except as an appearance in mind/body, and these come and go endlessly. Not one has any permanence at all. In knowing that, one does not cling to anything, and spontaneous Awareness is free of the relativity of reference points and bias.

This, is Freedom.

What must be seen is that no matter what is appearing on Awareness, is and can only be Awareness appearing as the energetic expression in forms and patterns.

Being aware of this is spontaneous and un-contrived. In essence, it is known already, yet because of beliefs, (beliefs in that which is appearing) this Knowing is translated into more patterns of belief for the mind.

Knowing is untouched by anything that is appearing. It is untouchable and ever present as the direct cognition of 'what is'. The energetic array of phenomena is nothing but Awareness.

You are this Awareness.

The appearance is this Awareness also. You are not separate from anything at all. Even concepts of exchange or transmission are just conceptual. If you are Awareness, how could you be separate from another Awareness?

The chair is Awareness, appearing to be a chair. No separation. Names and labels do not actually separate anything reflected in a mirror. It is the same on this side of the mirror. The mind only seemingly divides.

28

Disillusioned

Who is disillusioned?

To be disillusioned is commonly thought to be a negative state of mind. When all illusions are dissolved, the natural freedom shines of itself. How can that be negative?

Quote, from Nisargadatta: *"The nature of the Self is pure Awareness, pure witnessing, unaffected by the presence or absence of knowledge or liking. Have your being outside this body of birth and death and all your problems will be solved. They exist because you believe yourself born to die. Un-deceive yourself and be free. You are not a person."*

29

No Effort

Follow what I am saying, and see if it rings true. See if it rings true in this immediacy, in this actuality of present evidence.

If you follow with some close undistracted attention, something will most likely reveal itself.

First off, acknowledge that there is 'Knowing' happening spontaneously. It is not a question of directing the attention, or of any 'doing' to make this 'Knowing' happen. It is! It is not a matter of 'what' is known either, because everything that is 'known' is spontaneously replaced in the never-ending display of appearances in mind.

Try to hang onto a thought and see how long it stays. 'What is known' in the realm of words and images is simply objectification.

At the base, or source of all (of anything), there is a 'simplicity of Knowing', and this is happening quite spontaneously. This does not rely on you 'doing' anything at all.

Whether you consider that you are aware or not aware of THIS — it IS already so in its fullness as this immediate actuality. There is 'Knowing' and this is prior to any expression or belief of 'not Knowing' without exception.

One could say that it is timelessly present. Actually, this Knowing cannot be stopped. IT IS Timelessly expansive — Presence.

THIS can also be described as Ever-Present Clarity in which everything appears.

There has never been a 'time' when there has not been this Knowing. It is a fundamental aspect of immediate Presence, this clarity, irrespective of whatever appears in the mind. It is not 'personal'. It is also the very nature of existence and non-existence. It is the spontaneous and timeless nature of your own essential Being-ness.

A definite and thorough investigation reveals something quite different to the ordinary view. This can be discovered quite effortlessly.

With an un-contrived looking, it reveals itself so simply.

What I am saying is not based on 'belief' at all — it is a direct and immediate Knowing. In this investigation (here), there is a view that clearly shows that there is no 'me' or 'entity' (in any shape or form) 'here' that 'knows' or 'does' anything. Since it does not exist, or since it is only an appearance, it cannot 'see' or 'know' anything either.

Seeing is spontaneously happening, prior to any pattern that may appear in the mind. Patterns are seen, yet they do not compound into anything substantial.

Through this investigation, this naked Knowing, is freed from the superimposed concept of an individual that is commonly called a 'person'. Yet this freedom of 'Seeing – Knowing' has never actually been obscured. It only appears to be so, to a belief pattern called 'me' — a reference point!

There actually is no one to agree or disagree with this. Make no mistake about it, 'me' is simply 'mind content'.

Can a 'thought' see? No, of course not. The so-called 'me' is apparently a long standing habitual pattern in body and mind. Beyond this pattern the open clarity of vision is revealed to be immediate, timeless actuality, in which there can no longer be sustained an independent fixation or belief in being an 'entity'.

Belief can't stand on its own.

The behavior and speech, which is commonly attributed to an 'entity', will continue to appear and disappear. These appearances spontaneously appear in just the same way as all appearances appear. They appear and disappear in this timeless clarity that you are (I AM).

For those that sense a taste of freedom, with further exploration, it opens out and all that is false is spontaneously revealed. In the clarity of 'what is,' belief can't remain as the habitual troublesome 'bondage of self'.

Freedom is fully sensed as a vastness, an expansion, wherein the whole fabrication of a hypnotic 'belief system' falls apart with no effort being made by anyone.

Natural freedom dispels the erroneous bondage — as light dispels darkness.

For some, it may transpire that at some point the mind kicks back in with concepts about a practice for 'waking up'. Let it be seen for what it is. Like a creature venturing out of a hole, there may arise a panic, a running back for cover. Freedom is scary for the bonded conceptual belief system. As the 'venturing out' of habitual patterns expands, then the taste of real freedom spontaneously responds (in a manner of speaking).

The naked brilliance of 'what is' fills the Being-ness, and the limited views from 'a hole in the ground', drop away. A sense of relief may arise.

Self-shining Awareness reveals everything for what it is.

The apparent mirage of a constricted realm of erroneous beliefs, is exposed by this un-contrived simplicity.

This, is the true nature of mind — clear and empty. Non-conceptual-Seeing-Knowing.
When have you ever, truly, been anything with any lasting qualities 'other' than this Non-Conceptual- Seeing-Knowing?

You may notice how the mind attempts to divide what has been expressed into its usual dualistic realms. Non-Duality has no polar opposites. The habitual fixations of being someone who 'wants' to hang onto 'something' is unnecessary. All there is, is direct cognition.

Once this is seen clearly, the apparent power in the 'stories' of separation are over. The power that they appeared to have had for so long, is over. The roots of self-deception, like weeds, are ripped from their source of energy. Belief dissolves.

30

Radical Leap

There are an infinite number of ways to describe the situation that we find ourselves in — this applies to anyone, anywhere, at any moment, in space and time. Each description would have a beginning and an end. It would be limited. It would reveal a bias or a leaning and these would flex about within the realm of words.

Basically, it is all name and form in space and time. Space equates as 'distance', and time equates as 'duration'. However, all concepts are relative to reference points and find their meaning via referencing other concepts. This must be seen very clearly.

Let me suggest a radical leap, of mind, body, and faith, 'into' the Time-less NOW. No distance from HERE, and no TIME, other than THIS moment right NOW.

This very moment contains, ever so spontaneously, the ultimate description in space and time. This expression is an ephemeral notion of the ultimate form that is truly formless.

It is right in front of your eyes — right here, right now. This ultimate and immediate description is actuality, it is not a facsimile. It is actualized Awareness right now!

It is totally unlimited — whether there is a corporal Knowing of it or not.

There is no 'present' other than this ephemeral situation of Presence — now, as it always is.

There is nothing you can say that will add or subtract from this ever-fresh moment of actualizing Awareness. The immediate livingness is the 'I am-ness' in all things. It is nothing 'other' than this ultimate expression, this infinitely unique expression of right here, right now.

There is nothing else and nowhere else — just THIS.

Each moment is fresh and new. This moment has never happened before and yet it has never been divided into fragmented moments.

THIS, is truly ONE moment.

The subtleness of this timelessness is too subtle for the intellect. The intellect cannot explain the Being-ness. The Being is Self-contained. It needs no language. This is why the mind goes blank. Being shines of itself.

This moment is not conditioned by 'a past' — because this moment is all there is and ever is. In essence this moment is Un-born.

The only way to know this is right here, in the immediate, natural space of Knowing, which is timeless. *How* that is revealed is a mystery.

The apparent individualized mind is only a limited appearance in universal mind. These are concepts, not absolute truth.

Don't imagine other realms apart from your immediate Presence right now.

This bridge that spans the universal and the individual (which are really one) is the attention and it is this that appears as a means of Realization for the otherwise limited mind.

It is all Awareness, appearing as many. It appears as your life.

Pay attention to the natural state of clarity and realize your true nature of wakefulness.

Quote, from Sri Nisargadatta Maharaj: *"Reject the known. Welcome the unknown and reject it in its turn. Thus you come to a state in which there is no knowledge, only being, in which being itself is knowledge."*

31

Attuned

Seeing is spontaneously happening. That which is Seeing remains invisible. Everything that is seen appears and disappears without exception, while Seeing remains as it is.

You are Present and Aware. Do not assign your identity onto anything that is seen, not even onto this body, which you know as your own. Stay attuned to this spaciousness and remain free and open — as THAT which is 'Seeing – Knowing'. It is NOT conceptual!

You are this light of Knowing, which is prior to the body and mind.

Some say they can't see this truth. It can't be seen! It is the Seeing!

There is no such thing as 'Not Seeing'. All sentient Beings are Seeing. It is the very nature of Being. What appears in the Seeing is is-ness, and is-ness does not 'become' anything other than what it IS. There is no 'becoming' in Is-ness, or Being.

BE-ing. See-ing. Know-ing.

Ever Fresh and New.

Seeing, is prior to the image-form of any so-called 'SEER'.

'You' can't stop Seeing, just like you can't catch a train that has already left the station. Run as fast as you can, but you will not catch up with it. In other words, Seeing is the immediacy. The Seer is time bound. All the mind's interpretations are always 'after' the fact.

Nothing happens, yet every apparent happening is happening, NOW. The only time there is, is this immediacy we call 'now'. It is not 'somewhere else'. Everything is IMMEDIATE. All else is NOT. Yet we cannot affirm nor deny existence for any 'thing'.

All we know is that 'I AM'.

Wordless Presence cannot be negated. Is-ness is Seeing. Not two.

If this still does not register clearly with you, then simply acknowledge that Seeing is spontaneously happening.

32

Direct Experience

There is only ever direct experience-ING!

There are actually NO experiences!

There is only THIS, experiencing now. NOW!

Be open to this Presence that you are – be open without leaning upon any thought or concept. That is what everyone is seeking and missing – missing it because that activity of seeking is an active moving away from the simplicity of natural Presence - THIS clear thoughtless Presence, is IT!

33

Open

Can you completely open to THIS ever-fresh moment of Being Presence, without relying on words or conditioned mind?

Isn't this 'you' a concept?

Can a concept 'do' anything?

Is Openness conceptual?

It is a pure absence of concepts, untouched by any concept that may appear in or upon it.

Without 'doing' anything, is it possible to let all mind projections and processes drop away?

Contrivance in this, as in meditation techniques, is most common, and all 'results' are delusional for 'the believer', 'the doer'.

Is it simply an absence of all 'doing'?

A relaxation into effortless, simple Presence?

The ancient teachings tell us that Awareness is space-like. We can liken it unto space.

How can we directly experience this?

Drop all thought for a moment and let your natural Awareness be space-like.

Where is your authentic Presence — if not this natural Presence here right now?

Where is your absolute potentiality if not here now?

It is certainly not in the transient content of mind. The content of mind is unreliable and cannot be predicted with any assurance, unless we wish to rely on habitual notions.

'Who' is predicting?

It is the habitual notions that keep us conceptually enslaved in a false prison. Yet not one of them has any permanency. If there is a disagreement on this, it can only be a concept. It can be nothing but conflicting concepts.

What permanency does a concept or a thought have?

Your authentic Being is the natural, spontaneous, Presence, which is ever Present and ever prior to all the transient mind processes. The use of the word 'prior' is intended to reveal something unchanging in essence, yet appearing as all these changing aspects of Awareness or consciousness. Your (timeless) authenticity can never be reduced or confined into a (time bound) habitual process in the mind. No concept can ever truly re-present what is being pointed out because it is this ever-fresh Presence, in which nothing is truly attached to a past or future.. Omnipresent means All Presence.

In essence, the content is empty, and equal to the container. Not two. IT IS, whether there is a concept appearing within it (or about it), or not.

By its very nature, this moment, no matter how it appears, is ever fresh, ever immediate and that is truly all there IS.

It is recognised that all concepts of a past and a future are just conceptual flights of the mind. The only place they can appear is IN THIS moment of now. Release all grasping at 'things' that 'are not' within this living actuality. Some call this 'going on present evidence' (being equal with).

Simply be open.

Be open with the Presence of wakeful attention. It is natural. Make no extraneous efforts to 'do' or 'be' anything. The actuality of this natural

Presence is always prior to any considering that 'you do not have it' or 'that you do have it'. It is your natural Presence whether the 'you' of habitual mind 'has' this Presence of mind, or not. One could turn it around and say that IT has 'you'. Establish this Presence of mind in the immediate fact that this simple 'Knowing' is the actuality of Presence Awareness — ever prior to all mind content and all thoughts — even about this.

There is no need to ask, "What do I need to know beyond this Presence of Knowing?"

There is nothing before or beyond THIS. Everything is Clear and Obvious — within the natural scope of Awareness, right here, right now.

Pure Seeing is the first instant of cognition.

34

Intelligence

The essential message of the Vedas is that 'Ishwara', the pure intelligence, the vital life force, is the un-manifest inner-most 'I' called *Antaratman*, which is in all sentient Beings. Its nature is pure consciousness — Awareness.

It is the singular essence, the singular livingness of all Beings. It is not separated into 'parts', at all. It is the living spirit or life force, which pervades the entirety of all there IS.

Without this vital livingness, the body is a dead thing. It cannot see or know anything without this livingness, this intelligence. All the senses of the body and mind close down when this vital link is broken.

This singular Source animates all living creatures without ever entering into any realm of 'time' other than this moment.

The experience-er is a 'time bound', fictitious 'entity', and is simply a reflection from various, objectified 'reference points', in a dualistic mind (divided mind).

The multiplication of this Singular Essence is what we call creation.

The manifest arises from the un-manifest:

Shiva — Potency — The Un-manifest — static aspect of Awareness. Intelligence — Direct Cognition — Symbolized by Shiva having one eye open as he sleeps.

Shakti — The Manifest — The Active aspect of Awareness — Energy.

Together they are Intelligence-Energy.

ONE - not two! Pure Advaita.

Pure experiencing. This immediate intelligence of livingness, it is this immediate experience-ing which has no reference points at all. It needs none and has no 'place' to 'store' any, since this pure functioning is ceaselessly activated as this directness of Being.

All entities are seemingly created in 'time' and processes of mind. The whole manifestation is constantly resolving itself as this dynamic display of the elements we call 'the world'.

Nothing at all, in this mind realm of 'time', has any substantiality whatsoever apart from being an elongated belief system of concepts and ideas. These are accompanied by subsequent states, which appear to span or spread out into a time realm, which appears to support the belief system.

Here is the crux of it all: It is all nothing but experience-ing. Self-evident in direct cognition — which is timelessly present. This fact, when seen clearly, is a cutting through of the belief system of a 'person'. The 'personal' disappears in pure Knowing.

In the appearance of changing circumstances, only certain 'seekers' are attracted to this directness. The directness itself, resonates through them, dissolving them as it draws the attention to that which IS. This, is its wholeness. In other words, that which 'is not', the false, is revealed, and the bondage of self falls away like a discarded appendage.

35

Recognition

There will always be those that live completely in the natural and spontaneous life. It is referred to here, as the natural state. For some, it first appears as an instantaneous falling away of erroneous beliefs. For others, they are shown a living resonating example of this open and natural state. This recognition opens into direct cognition spontaneously.

Knowing, is this living intelligence that dissolves erroneous belief.

Even though one may believe that one is living in obscured mind stuff, the basis of one's true nature is right here, right now. It only appears to be smothered by troubles and beliefs. Seeing–Knowing, is ever here as the pure functioning of Presence Awareness — timelessly so.

36

Space of Knowing

Profound quote, from Ramana Maharshi :
"You impose limits to your true nature of infinite Being, then, you get displeased to be only a limited creature, then you begin spiritual practices to transcend these non-existing limits. But if your practice itself implies the existence of these non-existenting limits, how could they allow you to transcend them?"

There is really only one essential message that all the true teachers are pointing at. It arises from the innate freedom that they live spontaneously. The message is so simple, yet it is expressed in so many wondrous ways.

It delivers the attention back into 'space-like Awareness', 'the space of Knowing' which is direct, un-mediated cognition.

It is recognized that one cannot attain that which one truly already IS.
It is also spontaneously realized that there is nothing to 'do' to bring about some 'event' of

Awakening.

    Wakefulness is already here as Presence Awareness.

Your true nature is Self-Shining Awareness.

37

Chronologically Speaking

Time is a concept, which is useful in a worldly sense. Being a concept, it is simply a movement in mind. Time is duration. No beginning or end is really 'happening' anywhere, except in appearance.

We may apperceive that time is a movement, which appears in eternity. Eternal Stillness, Eternal Movement. The pulse of Self-Awareness. Just this, and nothing else.

This Eternal Present Moment may be called 'Eternity', and it can be understood to be Pure Duration.

No beginning, no end. Is-ness.

Everything changes and nothing changes, yet we must move on. As the saying goes, 'time waits for no man'.

Any chronological instrument (timepiece), no matter what it is made from, will never last in the pure duration of Eternity. The instruments very nature is energy and the nature of energy is to move. That is a concept but useful temporarily.

A chronological instrument can never encompass that which it is measuring. Just like a measuring tape cannot encompass what it is measuring, in all the dimensions. It is just held up against the 'object'. Eternity can equally be named as the timeless, expansive, Presence. No Thing.

This, is nothing other than this immediacy that we call life. Right Now.

If we transpose this 'understanding' onto the concept of Mind, we may see something equally illuminating.

All thoughts are transient appearances in Mind. In the pure duration of empty mind, they are nothing. They are a movement in stillness.

The true nature of mind is clear and empty. This, is the timeless nature of Eternal Mind – Awakened Mind – No Thing.

The limited view from an intellect can never capture or encompass the pure intelligence from which the intellect springs forth.

One Source. Undivided.

The Ultimate is here, now. It is the pure function of Seeing. It is the pure function of Knowing.

Not Two.

You are That.

38

Hammered

You may believe that you get caught up in 'things'. The 'entity', the 'you', that you may believe that you are, and the terrain of 'being caught', is all simply content of mind, along with associated habitual states in body and mind.

The nature of this image-ing (imagination) is just concepts, images, and belief. Without the energy of belief, it vanishes.

With a clear Seeing of this fact, you recognize that this Seeing is from outside of — or beyond 'that' which is seen. This reveals directly and immediately something which otherwise is difficult or even impossible to grasp through concepts. The mind appears to keep turning 'what is seen', along with what is imagined, into more concepts in a kind of internal dialogue or monologue —all stories — merely descriptions of the world. These are all habitual, associative, thought patterns.

Notice the fact that direct cognition never ceases — not even for an instant. You can't stop Seeing, just like you can't stop Knowing — And you can't stop Being.

Being - Seeing - Knowing are three aspects of natural Presence.

All the comings and goings are simply a conceptual flow, the 'content' in mind. Nothing is permanent in any of this content.

These points are hammered away at until it sinks in. When it sinks in, the words are just words as they always were. Like splitting a huge rock with wedges, shims and hammer blows. One must find a line in the grain of the rock. Place the wedges in a correct alignment. Many, many blows are needed as the force of the blows sinks into the rock. The grain splits in minute cracks. Then, the final blow may be the slightest tap and 'crack', it is done.

The only permanent aspects are Being and non-Being, which cannot be separated.

Seeing, hearing, tasting, smelling, touching, feeling, and thinking, all appear in this space of Knowing that you are. It's obvious.

This simple truth is a key point — profound, yet mostly bypassed.

What do you have to do to make any of these functions start working?

Are they not already fully here in the immediate

Being-ness? Spontaneous Being.

When have you not been this spontaneous Being-ness apart from some conceptual matrix? Even that appears spontaneously.

Contemplate this key point: Can you determine that there is or could ever be anything 'outside' of this immediate and direct cognition, this Knowing, of 'what is'? This view from the open nature of Empty Mind, is not a process of mind. There is no entity in that, only openness.

39

Stories

The story begins in Awareness and ends in Awareness. Awareness is not limited by anything whatsoever. There is 'no one' that knows this.

There is Knowing!

All entities are simply content of mind, they have no substantiality beyond the nature of a mirage. This is an outrageous suggestion to make to a 'person'.

These words are appearing in Awareness just like any of the myriad thoughts that appear in your own mind.

Do you make thoughts happen?
Are thoughts yours?
How do 'you' make thoughts?
What are thoughts made of?
What history do thoughts have that are valid without more thoughts being added?

It is all patterns appearing.

When we really look into it, when we examine closely what is actually happening, we find something beyond all our conditioning and habitual views and expectations.

The point is: 'Who' thinks and 'Who' is 'doing'?

Do you, as a creature of belief, really believe that you are an independent 'thing' that has power to determine anything at all?

Are these things what they appear to be?

Did you determine the limits of your organic nature? Can you leave this planet?

How far can you go out in space without a life support system? — and when any support system fails, what happens?

The continued belief in 'the erroneous' is all that appears to keep the mind in a (discontinuous) sense of a separation — and in a time realm.

A realm of forgetting and remembering is a realm that appears to exclude the clear and obvious Presence of what is. This mind realm is conceptual and that includes what is written here or anywhere else. These words are an attempt at pointing back or cutting through to 'that' which is Seeing — 'that' which is Knowing — IN YOU.

This immediate Knowing is not some state of

mind to acquire! It is already Present — simply direct cognition. Direct Knowing. It does not rely on the past!

Intellectuals argue about all manner of conceptual baggage. What is achieved?

In the appearance of history, of 'time' there have been hundreds of years of learned men and women with untold numbers of books of knowledge. Has anything really changed?

The big questions remain unanswered because they have no definitive answers.

From the open view of Empty Mind, with no attachment or detachment, everything is clear and obvious just as it IS.

Has your immediate Knowing of the so-called 'world' been contaminated by anything?

Isn't the view clear — crystal clear?

Isn't it clear and free of all words, theories, and empty of any need of a secondary thought or image?

Without any thought having to be projected onto it, isn't it direct and immediate? Clearly it is so. In pure Seeing, it is so. In pure Knowing, it is so.

40

Singular

Our singular identity is authentic Being.

It is Self-shining Presence. It is complete and untouched by delusion. It is ever Present as this first instant of Knowing.

The pure and direct functioning of all your senses are not removed from this authentic Being in any way. Everything registers in direct cognition, just as it is.

The in-authentic Being is 'thought based' only and is merely identification, a fixation with thoughts and images. They have no substantial Being whatsoever. This in-authentic Being is an appearance, a reflection. It is like a reflection of the moon in the still waters of a lake. There is no independence in it at all. It is an image only. If the Sun (authentic Being) was not in the sky, then the moon would not shine and it could not appear as a reflection in the lake at all.

Amidst all the activities of the endless and changeful nature of life, this motionless authentic Being remains pure and untouched.

It is Self-Knowing Awareness. It is not attainable, simply because it already IS.

Due to belief in mere reflections and shadows, the mind raises doubts about itself. By not giving them any weight, they resolve themselves quite naturally.

Can the Oneness of things be divided without a thought? Thought actually divides nothing at all, except itself. Oneness is clear and obvious and it can never be divided except as a conceptual division in mind. Your authenticity is in your own natural completeness, just as you are.

Stay with the warmth of the resonation of authenticity in yourself. Watch what happens. In the warmth of this Presence, a doubt is like a cool and pale shadow.

In simply paying attention, let your own light of 'Seeing and Knowing' spontaneously cut through the façade of all erroneous beliefs. It is not a 'doing' and cannot be contrived. It is not by any habitual, spiritual, 'effort maker', based on past merits. Such things are merely more obstacles. No one can be told 'how'. It is an aspect of a pure resonance in authentic Presence which brings it to the fore.

41

Erroneous Bondage

Is there a psychological 'stance', or mental resistance to this obviousness? It can't be that simple? YES it IS!

If it is clear now, then what 'problem' could you ever wish to bring back into this clarity?

If there is a problem you wish to bring into this clarity, then see it for what it is. Its nature will also be clear and obvious. It could be said that this 'problem' is the very fabric that you should examine closely, because in the 'fabric' of this problem, lies the bondage that you wish to be free of.

No one else can know it as intimately as yourself.

It is your erroneous bondage, and to be free of it, you must look and see for yourself in this clarity that you ARE. Do not be tempted to postpone this, because if you don't see it NOW — when will you see it?

Investigate. Investigate, until the stories all fall apart and leave this ever Present Knowing, simply shining through the mind.

This clarity will remain just as it is, whether you continue on with your erroneous beliefs or whether you see through them.

The only difference is in psychological stance, which includes all beliefs and suffering. I will ask the question again. What problem would you wish to bring into this clarity?

The essence that you truly are, is free right here in this direct or immediate actuality. THIS, is all there is. What is the doubt in this?

In this direct view, there is an open view from empty mind. This is so, whether you believe it or not. Even if there is a lot of activity going on in the mind, the clarity is there, and what's more, it is obvious, so obvious that you miss it. You miss it because of a habitual need of a concept to hang onto. It is not a concept! It is non-conceptual Awareness which knows all concepts — this **Knowing Presence is your true nature.**

Pure Seeing, pure Knowing, is non-conceptual Awareness.

What concept can you make 'that' into? Words are just words, and Knowing is Knowing, and is ever prior to words and concepts.

It IS clear, and it has 'always' been clear. It is this vast, immediate clarity, in which all manner of 'things' only appear to be.

It is only the content of mind, erroneous beliefs and habitual attachments which seemingly cloud this clarity— for the fixating individualized consciousness.

All there IS, is Self-Knowing Awareness— direct and immediate cognition. The space of Knowing.

THAT, you ARE.

FEEL the space in which the body appears in. The direct light of illumination is nothing but your own true nature.

Self-shining Awareness. It shines through the mind content and illuminates everything, without distinction.

This light dissolves fixations in mind.

Quote from Sri Nisargadatta Maharaj: *"There is no reality in your comings and goings and your problems are so unreal"*.

42

Investigate

Investigate — that is all that is necessary.
Investigate in the immediate space of Knowing.

From this space of immediate Knowing, all is just appearing and disappearing. And what's more, nothing can touch you because you are this immediate, clear and empty, timeless space, of Knowing.

I am not spouting some elaborate learned and stored knowledge here. There is actually no one here that knows anything. It is ALL immediate Knowing. This immediacy of Knowing is simply the natural openness of Presence Awareness. From this direct experiencing here, the appropriate words appear in an expression of or about that direct experiencing. I am the formless space of Knowing. All grasping consciousness and afflictive emotions are in time, and 'time' is Mind.

When you return the mind to its true nature, which is clear emptiness, all these elongated time bound 'things' vanish. There is nothing for them to attach to. No entity there. There is no 'time' for them to exist IN.

43

Ever Fresh View

This 'eternal Presence' is right here as this first instant of Awareness. It never budges from this.

You do not have to 'go' anywhere or 'do' anything to 'get' anything, regarding the natural freedom of this eternal fact.

This eternal Presence is appearing to be obscured in those that have a firm belief in erroneous concepts, — 'me' — concepts of being a separate individual, a 'person'. It is a stream of conceptualizing, which revolves around and through a series of beliefs. This holds the attention in a cyclic fashion. It often appears as confusion. Slipping from one concept to another, keeps the mind busy with its endless stories of a 'me' and the 'other'.

This can only ever contain brief 'passing' moments of satisfaction, since the very vulnerability of its foundation is due to it being merely a belief and not a fact.

'Build your house on the rock — do not build it on the sand' — from my Sunday School lessons at the age of 6. Any unexpected 'thing' can come along and disturb the 'me's' shaky eccentricity.

Sound familiar? Moments of peace from such cyclic mind activity ends without notice, as we appear to slip back into more concepts. All this is in the appearance of the 'normal' life of an individual.

'We', as a fixation in mind, are continually 'going with' what the mind throws up, like a bee to a flower. Just like rainwater flows in old pathways in the virgin soil, it is just a habit, yet it brings so much trouble for the one who believes in it.

It does not have to be a cloud of unKnowing.

Beyond all such activities in mind, the eternal Presence of the natural state, (our true nature) is right here, right now, fully Present and unobstructed. Seemingly hidden, so it seemingly reappears.
Natural Awareness is Presence.

It is clearly obvious, yet by so many it is not noticed at all because of its non-objective nature.

All the functioning senses are registering everything just as it is — in the immediacy of this ever-Present moment. This subtle fact is a mostly unrecognized key to Self-Realization. Yet it is so obvious — this moment now — is all there is! Can you know this fully right now? It is so obvious. You are That. How can you say you do not know this?

Right now, without going into some time realm in mind — it is obvious, neither affirmation nor denial can touch its ever- Present ephemeral actuality.

We apparently move into some state of mind where we deny this obvious moment of clarity. By resting in this openness, (which includes the immediate registration of 'what is'), the mind is thoroughly known — and known without doubt, to be clear and empty. This is the place where Awareness and mind are indistinguishable.

The content of mind appears and disappears in the same way that all things appear and disappear in the manifestation. The apparent difference is only in scale.

All happens in this Knowing Presence that you are. With a fine attention, it can be seen that the mind is filled, yet emptied, in one instant.

By not fixating on anything at all, this boundless Awareness is known to be free and obviously so.

Nothing of the activity in mind compounds

into anything at all. The universal aspect of mind--pure mind, awakened mind--remains open. It only appears to close for the fixating individual mind. The curtains are drawn and so the open view is shut off for the 'me' and its manifold reference points.

This immediate openness is full of Knowing yet ever empty.

Knowing includes a direct and clear 'sensation' that there is 'no one' here (as a fixation) in this openness. This Presence Awareness is undeniable and not negotiable! It is totally Present with no flavor of positive or negative at all. It just is.

It is Self-shining, Self-Knowing Awareness.

It may very well be, that you still imagine that you will solve all your problems somehow. Some method or belief system will save you from chaos and suffering. How can it be that these problems can be solved? They are no more than a mirage. You can transcend them but not through belief or concepts — only through direct Knowing — non-conceptual Awareness.

Consider this: What do you actually 'do' at the moment of Seeing through a mirage? Does it not spontaneously reveal its nature without any 'doing' on your part? All these problems are simply incomplete views, full of preferences and bias. They are partial views of 'what is'. They belong to an erroneous view. The one that thinks it sees a problem is indicatively embedded in the fixated view of 'the seer' — mind content which can't see at all!

Pure Seeing is Non-Dual — there is no 'seer', no substantial object that is 'seen' as distinct from the pure function of Seeing.

All these delineations of wholeness can only be added to by the mind with more delineation.

Pure, unadulterated Seeing, cuts through all of this. See clearly that none of these apparent additions actually stay or 'hang around'. All these delineations are like lines drawn onto a clean sheet of paper.

If you continue to be these fixations in mind, all you end up with is a sheet covered with lines, words and theories. Chaos and confusion, or conversely, a nice pattern. The paper, the lines and the one making the scrawling details are all appearing in the clean and empty space of impartial, Self-Knowing Awareness.

Drop all internal dialogue and 'come back' to the ever-Present first instant of Presence Awareness. For one moment, stay open and simply be the Seeing. In this way everything is revealed.

Stay open in the vastness of THIS.

Note: Common meditation is a relative means, like anything else, of Self-discovery--The discovery of this undifferentiated natural state of pure Awareness with all its appearances on, or in That, which IS this Awareness.

44

Shining Through the Mind

Natural Wakefulness — Awakened Mind.

The skeptical nature of the intellect is a bit of a hurdle for many. Even with a strong interest in this subject, they continually miss the clarity and significance of direct Seeing prior to the intellectual processes.

This message is an introduction via many subtle and simple pointers to our natural stateless state of wakefulness. The text draws the attention back to a space of direct Knowing.

This direct Knowing is yours. It cuts through all dogma and belief systems. What is, is Present Evidence.

This natural wakefulness is fully Present in everyone — irrespective of all beliefs and inadvertence.

Awareness is what you are. You cannot increase or diminish it in any way.

Awareness IS — all there is.

Doubts about this arise from a dualistic mind set — such doubts do not change the ever-Present FACT of wakefulness itself. The doubt appears in mind, and registers in pure Awareness – wakefulness – otherwise you would not know of it at all. This wakefulness can appear to be more or less Present to the identified consciousness.

However, this 'mind processing' is not actually Seeing or Knowing anything. It is a process of re-cognizing — from 'past' images and impressions.

By contemplating the points raised, the mind may 'return' to its natural open clarity.

One must gently navigate through the erroneous beliefs and realize the ineffable qualities of Awareness. The habitual and dull pain of a false separation from wholeness, and a long-standing belief system inhibits a clear view.

This clouded view can be cleared away.

Love of Being — is the bridge, which spans this erroneous separation. We can simply open to the warmth of our own Being and stay quietly attentive.

With a simple open view, you may very well see clearly that you have never been bound, and that this innate freedom is yours.

You may also realize that this has always been the case. Few believe in such a possibility. It is not about belief!

It is a 'direct Knowing' of the fact. The fact of Being. 'Being' is present tense, it is always Now! What is it that is shining through the mind?

Awareness shines through the mind and illuminates all therein, without exception.

45

Enlightenment

Chop wood, carry water? Forget it.

There is no 'before' Enlightenment. There is no 'after' Enlightenment.

There is no Enlightenment 'other' than this moment. The light by which you see, is it.

THIS Presence.

All there is, is THIS — this immediate Knowing — right now. It is direct cognition. Pure Knowing.

There is no such thing as indirect cognition, it is All That. Knowing is all that is happening. Everything else is appearing and disappearing, in that Knowing.

You can call it Enlightenment if you wish, yet it will make no difference whatsoever.

You ARE this Knowing Presence - That is all.

46

Flow

In your apparent 'journey' you must find what is called 'a true teacher'. One who lives the freedom spoken of.

Time does not play a role in Self-Realization, so in the appearance, it can be very quick. Very quick - it is in fact, instantly revealed.

You must find out what it is that 'seemingly' obscures this clear Presence of immediate Knowing. Even though the messenger will tell you that there is no teacher and no teaching, you must pursue the situation to its final ending.

Paradoxically, such an 'ending' can only ever be 'a dissolution' of erroneous beliefs, right here, right NOW.

You are already HERE 'in' and AS this Moment. Prior to the concept 'moment' or 'time'. Get the message and be done with seeking all together.

"Free man, woman, move on." — George Adie.

Be free - move on. Don't fixate upon anything.

Let everything flow in its own natural way.

Quote, from Sri Nisargadatta Maharaj: *"Self-identification with the body creates ever-fresh desires and there is no end to them — unless this mechanism of bondage is clearly seen."*

47

See - Know - Be

SEE— what is real - in your life.
KNOW— what is real - in your life.
BE— what is real - in THIS immediate LIFE.

Then all these troublesome mind games will leave as if by their own volition.

THIS, IS IT.

Use this natural power of discrimination. See the true and see the false and KNOW the difference.

Don't waste time with paraphernalia or the problems of others. What you need is not on some 'shelf' somewhere or in some book. Nor is it in a teacher or guru.

What you are is all that you need.

Just pay attention. That is all. The rest takes care of itself.

Quote, from Sri Nisargadatta Maharaj: *"It is the very nature of illusion to dissolve on investigation. Investigate — that is all."*

Epilogue

No Seeker Can Get Here

The search for truth in 'oneself' is unnecessary! — Useless!!

It is the mindset of 'looking' which takes the mind on a never ending 'journey' to nowhere.

The authentic Being is not removed from the pure function of the senses. The senses do not 'lie' in the immediacy of their touch. What the mind translates from them may well be a gross distortion. The seeker is apparently caught in a realm of these mind translations and projections. 'It' thinks that 'it' is seeing. — It is not seeing at all. One could say that it is 'looking', but it isn't even doing that.

The seeker is nothing more than a reflection, an apparition which 'feeds' off the livingness.

You do not need to search for your own authenticity. Such seeking is just more reflections and delusion. How many 'steps' do you need to take to arrive at your authenticity? How many miracle courses?
— Surely None!

Drop the habitual seeker mind postures, those grasping notions, and let the mind rest from its incessant neediness, it's 'reactive' conceptualizing.

There is nothing to be afraid of in your true nature. It's **what you are not** that is so imaginary, fearsome AND fearful in its dualistic realm of mind stuff.

Let the mind rest on nothing. Let it be spacious. A living openness.

Watch — See — Natural Seeing is spontaneously here.

A series of re-actions may come up with an uneasy feeling in the chest. Let it be just as it is.

Reaction attracts reaction — and 'before you know it', there is a 'community' of angels and devils fighting for centre stage (in the psyche).

Rest in the empty space of direct cognition, in which all and everything is appearing. Be nothing at all.

Know immediately that the pure function of Seeing is free of what is seen. It is not above or below it. In a certain way, it is beyond it all.

The authentic pure Knowing is the only

accessor to pure Seeing. — No seeker can go there. — Why? — Because the seeker is just composed of thoughts and thoughts can't SEE.

There is no 'not Seeing'. See or recognize that this Seeing is already happening. Totally pure and direct. — It is what you ARE. —You are nothing other than That!

In this Seeing, there is direct information — 'intelligence' which is potently informative. By resting in this manner, the grasping, identified habitual consciousness is starved of its habitual 'feed'.

Like a cut vine, it will shrivel up and drop away.
This 'direction' given here is far more valuable than a hundred years of meditation or laborious practices.

The problem appears to be that it is all far too simple and far too effective.

There is no 'value' in it for the egoistic seeker.

It is far too effective in removing the grounds of erroneous belief. That is why this so-called 'teaching' of Non-Duality, will never be popular.

A lifetime of investment in the ego is just too much to give up, even for absolute freedom. It is really not an issue, except for an elusive self-image called 'me'.

How can a mirage have an issue?

Enough is enough.

Quotes, from Sri Nisargadatta Maharaj: *"When you are stabilized in your own Self, then there is no otherness, you are everything. If you abide in yourself, you are like space and there is no duality left. You are as expansive and as subtle as space, and that is liberation. You are not conditioned by name and form. If you are like space, what is the point of going elsewhere? The space, which is here, is also everywhere else."*

"Not becoming anything is the accuracy of our effort"
Sri Siddharameshwar Maharaj

Editor's Note

Many books have been written on the subject of Non-Duality, and while a majority of them speak about it in at least a similar fashion, you won't find the usual here.

When asked to write a forward for this book, I wondered how to add to such a masterpiece. No words can express rightfully, the validity and immediate clarity of seeing--knowing that this book reveals.

Continue to read the book, and read it yet again. The revealing will 'happen'--but only because it is already so.

I am grateful to Gilbert for coming out of his silent time to express these words. It took a little urging, but wow, the light that shines cannot be hidden.

--Julie Rumbarger

NOTES

NOTES

NOTES

NOTES

Self Aware

NOTES

Self Aware

NOTES

Made in the USA
Columbia, SC
25 April 2019